A Caring Christmas

John Evans

ISBN: 1505901308
ISBN-13: 978-1505901306

Contents

Forword

This is my second book looking at the role of a Carer. I have been caring for my mother for almost three years now but it is only in the past two weeks that this role has involved my entire family.

I care for my mother who suffered a severe stroke. As a result of this she lost the use of her left side and was left with complex pain issues. She requires full time care for all of her needs. In the first instance I was forced to leave my family while I cared for my mother at her home in Scotland. After two years of this I finally managed to bring my mother to the midlands where she stayed in a nursing home for around ten months while I sorted our housing situation. Finally, after nearly three years, my mother moved in with me and my family. This was December 2014, so now, for the first time in three years I was looking at a real family Christmas with all of my key family members under one roof.

I should mention that I have a partner and five year old son. They both suffer from a genetic condition called Myotonic Dystrophy. My partner has a less severe form than my son, as such she is his official carer. This complicates the family dynamics in quite a profound way. In the two years I was looking after my mother in Scotland my partner had a difficult time looking after herself and our son. I was away from the home for up to eight weeks at a time and she missed my presence and support. It was nice then to finally have us all together.

Having written my first book "Caring For Mum" and received some very good feedback from it I felt there was still more that I had to say on the subject of caring for an elderly and disabled parent. One of the things that kept coming back to me was the frequency people would ask how I am doing? It is a largely irrelevant question to my mind and I don't mean that in a nasty way. It is a conventional question born out of a genuine interest in my welfare, unfortunately, were I to provide a detailed and accurate answer it would be beyond most people. The simple fact is that, unless you are personally involved in a situation like mine then, with the best will in the world, you can't really understand what is involved. To my mind a part of the reason for that is that there is precious little material in the world for people to read, understand and learn about the role of a Carer. That is what this book is all about.

For seven days I kept a recorded diary of my day to day activities, my thoughts and feelings at the time events were taking place. I carried a Dictaphone with me the whole time and at regular times during the course of each day I recorded what transpired. Essentially this book is a transcription of those recordings. I have not edited them in any way except to remove individual names. As I have transcribed these diary entries I have also taken the opportunity to reflect and elaborate on some of the thought processes these entries touch upon.

I deliberately chose the seven day period that included Christmas day. I felt it was important to enable my audience to contrast and compare my experiences of this week with their own recollections of how they spent their week. It is my hope that at the end of this diary you, the reader, will have gained a greater understanding of what it really means to be a full time Carer.

Day 1

22nd December 2014

06:00am

"I'm the first one in the house to be up. As I come downstairs I can hear the little man starting to stir which means I've got maybe thirty or forty minutes before he's going to be screaming for attention. My partners alarm went off. That bloody tune from "Frozen", "Let It Go", it's really starting to wind me up. Not the best start to the morning, but without the alarm I wouldn't have moved today.

I come downstairs and it's cold, bitterly cold. I turn the heating up, then into the kitchen to make a cup of tea and the jobs start lining themselves up in front of me. I was too tired to do the washing up last night so I've got that waiting for me this morning. I've got the laundry that needs to go into the drier. I've got the Occupational Therapist coming at eight o'clock to co-ordinate with the care team and double check that all the equipment is working as advertised.

archetypal lounge lizard, milk in one hand, T.V. remote in the other, stretched out on the sofa while I move off into the kitchen and start work."

08.00am

"The Carers have arrived, I've given them the run down on the day, highlighted what's going to be happening today and, after a conversation with mum we decided that, although it's Monday, we're going to treat today like a Sunday and mum is going to have a day of bed rest. She's tired, she's had a big week. She's been up in her wheelchair all last week and that's tiring for her. This is one of the things I constantly have to balance out. Yes, I want mum to have as much interaction with the family and our life as possible. I want her to have a social life. I want her to feel involved. But at the same time, I have to recognise that mum is no longer as physically strong as she used to be. The stroke has affected her in quite a profound way, physically speaking. She tires easily and I have to let her dictate what she is capable of doing to a large extent.

Today is also a little bit unusual. We have the Occupational Therapist around. These are periodic visits to check that everything is working the way it is supposed to be, that niggling issues about the environment have been sorted to our satisfaction. Things like an increased turning circle in the kitchen for the wheelchair, making sure that the door thresholds are at the right level to allow comfortable wheelchair access. All of these kind of things. So she is now checking in with the care team with mum to make sure that the equipment that we have got up there is fit for purpose, is doing the job it is supposed to, that mum is happy with it, that the carers are happy operating it. So yes, this is an unusual event, but it makes no difference to the timing of the day.

Once the carers are finished then it will be time to get mums' breakfast. While the carers are up there getting mum ready I'll be down here getting my son changed, getting his nappy changed, get him cleaned up and into some fresh clothes and getting him ready for the day.

And my partner is still in bed."

So, my son is five years old and still in nappies. Terrible isn't it? The fact is that this is not laziness on the part of neither my partner nor myself. It is, in point of fact, a side effect of the Myotonic Dystrophy. The condition causes developmental delays, both physically and mentally. In my sons case one of the manifestations of this is his awareness of his bodily functions and his communication abilities. The only time my son has any awareness of his bodily functions is when he is constipated, which is a distressingly regular occurrence due to poor muscle function in his small bowel. Everything else is completely beyond his awareness. Toilet training is something people really take for granted. I don't think most people recognize just what a complex concept this is to put across to a child under normal circumstances. In this household, there are no normal circumstances however. We can only communicate basic concepts to our son due to his low word stock for a child his age and the fact that the majority of communication is conducted via Makaton sign language. So our son is still in nappies and this situation is likely to remain for some time to come. Effectively we are being led by our son in this regard. As his communication skills improve and his awareness of himself improves I am confident we will eventually reach a point where toilet training will yield positive results, until then we have no choice but to continue as we are.

I have also been making a point to note my partners sleep patterns. This is in no way intended to be taken as a negative statement. I am simply highlighting one of the issues my partner faces as a direct result of the Myotonic Dystrophy. She suffers excessive fatigue. Left to her own devices she could probably sleep the entire day away. She is on daily medication for this aspect of the condition and without it we would be in serious trouble.

09:00am

"The carers have been and gone. The Occupational Therapist has been and gone. Both groups are extremely happy with how things are progressing. The Occupational Therapist is really happy with the way mum is, how much better she is looking now that she's home. It was a nice glowing report which kind of underscores the need for bringing mum home.

With the best will in the world a care or Nursing Home cannot provide everything that a person needs in their life. They have neither the time, resources, knowledge or, in some cases, inclination.

Now that they've all gone it's time for breakfast, so I've taken mums breakfast up to her, a cup of tea, refreshed her water, made sure she's got everything she needs for a little while. I've woken my partner up, she's a slow starter in the morning."

11:30am

After getting my partner up and moving I gave her a couple of instructions about things I needed to be done. Drying to take out of the washing machine and folded and put away, you know, just basic things like that, look after mum, and I decided I'd take myself out for an hour and go and visit a friend for coffee, something I very, very rarely do. But I needed it, I needed the chance to talk and vent to someone who might understand what's going on in my head. While it doesn't remove the frustrations, it helps me relieve the tensions that they cause. A necessary thing.

Of course, then I come back and yeh, my partner has taken the washing out of the dryer, folded it, left it piled up in

the kitchen and that's about it. She went up and checked on my mum, left an empty breakfast bowl up there and an empty cup, didn't bother clearing anything away. It's like unless I write instructions down with details she never switches her brain on. I'm dealing with three children in this house, it's as simple as that. Unless I give detailed instructions to every one of them, nothing gets done and that's really starting to get to me now. It's got nothing to do with whether I love the person or not, I need them to start taking initiative over their own lives, and they're not which just adds to my work load.

So, I'm back now. I'm just having a quick cigarette and a cup of tea and then I'm going to make mums' lunch. I've already made her a cup of tea, gone up and checked her out.

I've had some parcels arrive for her today. Some new bras, yeh, that's an odd thing isn't it? Buying bras for your mum. The things I could say about that concept. Some bibs, interesting disparity between the two items there, both intensely personal but in widely different ways. And mums had another Christmas card from an old friend of the family."

Looking back at this entry it is clear that some of the thoughts I was having towards my partner at this time were less than charitable. Anyone who knows me knows that I do not class myself as a nice person. I am irritable, set in my ways, something of a pedant and at times altogether unpleasant. Hey, I'm bi-polar, what do you want from me?

The thing is, while I recognize that my partner has difficulties in the areas of energy and motivation and that these difficulties stem from her condition, I can only make allowances so far. I've said all along that I would never expect my partner to pick up any of the personal care duties involving my mum but I did expect her to do her fair share of the up-keep of the house. This was agreed long in advance of my mum coming home. So now that mum is home it seems my partner has just shut down and that frustrates me.

I love her but I cannot be expected to do the entirety of the work in this house without some support.

01:15pm

> ***"The Carers have been and gone for the lunchtime session. Mum was fairly easy today because she hadn't got out of bed so it's just a check to see if she needed any cleaning up or any attention that I couldn't provide, any of the personal care stuff, so it was relatively quick and easy today.***
>
> ***I'm now gonna put my head down and rest for a bit. I don't normally do this but this past week's been a challenging one. I've been suffering with a lot of pain. I've been on heavy duty pain killers so my sleep patterns have been virtually non-existent and I'm running on a massive sleep deficit. After the carers had gone mum decided she wanted to grab a nap so, with my partner and son safely looking after each other downstairs, I've decided to try and do the same for an hour or two. I can't go any longer than three o'clock though because I've got to get back up and get food cooked for this evening for us all.***
>
> ***Thankfully my partner helped out and finished off the remainder of the washing up for me otherwise that would have been another task I would have had to do before I could even think about any rest. So that's been a big help"***

In many ways caring for an aged parent in my mothers' condition has similarities to caring for a baby or young child. Finding time to rest is incredibly important. When possible a mother will try to align her rest periods with those of her baby and that is exactly what I try and do here. Tiredness is the constant enemy. The days can be very long and unexpected events can extend those days without warning so it is important to get as much rest as you can whenever you can. For anyone this is important. Excessive fatigue can lead to potentially dangerous mistakes. But for me it is even more important due to my bi-polar and diabetes. Tiredness makes me incredibly short tempered and impatient and this is not an environment which responds well to those conditions.

03:50pm

> ***"So, I got woken up at ten past three. I'm feeling a lot better, more refreshed after that little two hour catnap. I checked straight in on mum, got her a fresh cup of tea and a mince pie as a little pre-dinner treat. I've changed the T.V. channel for her, found something more enjoyable for her to watch.***
>
> ***I've caught up on my e-mails, had a cup of tea myself, now it's time to start thinking about the evening meal. Tonight we've got Spaghetti Bolognaise, well a Bolognaise Sauce with pasta. I don't like cooking spaghetti, I can't stand it. It's irritating stuff to deal with, it goes everywhere except in the mouth. It's a simple dish, but it's filling, it's got everything we need in it and, to be honest I've been cooking really intensely for the past week since mum came home so I'm just keeping it nice and chilled out and simple tonight, nothing too complex."***

Cooking is a constant challenge for me. I have opted to cook my mothers' meals instead of contracting that out to an external service. This is for two main reasons. Firstly, I feel we have enough strangers coming and going on a daily basis, any more and it could quickly become confusing and intrusive. Secondly it is allowing me to make sure that there is regular meal times with home cooked food for all of the family. I think this is really important for my sons' development, both in a social context but also in terms of his association with food. Currently he is a very picky eater and we have a lot of challenges getting him to eat what I would call, healthy food. This is a constant concern for me so my hope is that, by instituting a consistent and recognizable routine we can gradually encourage better eating habits with our son.

05.00pm

> ***"Three adults have been fed while my son predictably decided to turn his nose up at the food again. Giving him solid food is seriously challenging. He's ended up working himself into such a state he's gone to bed and had an early night. I hate it when he gets like this. All he does is cry and you've got no idea what he wants. He's five years old and he can't tell you what he wants, he can't tell you if there's anything wrong, he just sits and cries at you and everything you try he says no to and it's just frustrating in the extreme. At the end of the day it's not what you need. I mean I'm nearly twelve hours into my day. So he's gone to bed early in the hopes that he will calm himself down and settle down and he'll be a bit brighter tomorrow. Although the odds are good he's going to wake up now at around two o'clock in the morning, thirsty, which means any hope of a decent sleep pattern for me has just gone out of the window again because my partner won't wake up. But we'll see how it plays out."***

Like I said, my son is a picky eater and when he doesn't want food he cannot be forced. There's no point in trying. He immediately works himself up into such a state, screaming and crying. It is maddening. The communication difficulties really come to play at times like this and I get really frustrated with the whole situation. There are times I just have to walk away from it completely otherwise I run the risk of completely losing it myself, which really is not a good idea.

As for sleeping, my partner sleeps the sleep of the dead. Really, a brass band could march through our room at night and she would barely stir. Not me, however. If a pin were to drop in the street I would be awake instantly regardless of how tired I was when I went to bed. This means naturally I am the one to get up if our son stirs in the night.

09:00pm

"The Carers were in at seven and settled mum down. I went back up, took her a cup of tea, gave her the medication and a late night snack, she has a passion for shortbread so, why not?

Mum's not been feeling too good today and I finally realised what, potentially, the issue is. Mum needs a B12 injection basically. They are repeatable every twelve weeks or so and when mum is getting to the end of a cycle her energy levels and conscious levels drop, her ability to focus drops.

So my task for tomorrow is to phone the doctor and see how we are doing there, also I need to phone the District Nurses to get night bags for my mum because apparently we have one left. So tomorrow is already shaping up to be an eventful day. I've got delivery of a new sling coming and to be honest I'm not sure if mum is going to be feeling up to getting out of bed tomorrow. We'll see.

There's an awful lot of reasoning to be done with my mother. While her cognitive processes function quite well, she has a tendency to overthink things and little issues suddenly become major dramas for my mother. The problem is she has too much time to think and, unfortunately, a lot of the thinking is not constructive. That is something I need to address. I need to provide her with ways to direct her thinking in a manner that is constructive and productive for her. One of the new challenges.

I've turned mums light off now, left her with the T.V. on for a little bit while she finishes off her tea and biscuits and, when my partner goes to bed I'll go up and turn the T.V. off, and there we go. And that will be another day with mother. But for me, the day is not over."

10:40pm

" I'm going to be going to bed soon, I've just got two jobs left to do. My partner went to bed about an hour ago. I turned the T.V. off for Mum and settled her down about the same time. The little one, predictably, had woken up. He needed some milk, some comfort, I don't think that's going to be the first time tonight, but we'll see. So I made him up a bottle of milk, took it up to him, snuggled him back into bed, gave him lots of hugs and kisses, we'll see if he settles down.

I've just got to upload these files now, ready for transcription, wrap my partners Birthday present and then I'm going to turn in. Even though I had that nap this afternoon I'm still exhausted. I can barely keep my eyes open again. I've got a headache forming so I might take myself some Ibuprofen before I go to bed, just to take the edge off it and allow me to sleep, before it becomes a fixture behind my eye which is where my headaches tend to go. I'm tired. Good night."

It is easy to think that my day could have ended sooner than it actually did. The evening, however, bears similarities to the morning for me. Just as I need that hour of alone time in the morning before I face the day with my family, so too do I need that time at the evening in order to wind down.

I am one of those unfortunate people whose brain never seems to stop. It runs constantly at a million miles an hour and this means that sleep comes very hard to me. There is absolutely no point in my going to bed until my brain has slowed down enough for me to sleep. The net result of this is that I average between four and six hours of sleep a night, and that is completely dependent upon the good will of my family. If either my mother or my son has a difficult and restless night, then so will I.

Day 2

23rd December 2014

06:00am

> ***" I didn't really want to get up today. The moment I stepped out of my bedroom door I could hear Mum through one door, she's already awake. As I come downstairs my sons' door opens, light comes streaming out, he's already awake. In fact the only person who doesn't seem to want to start the day is my partner, bless her. My son willing, I'll let my partner sleep again, as long as I can.***
>
> ***I am hungry this morning. I feel like I ate like a horse yesterday but I'm still hungry. I'm trying to lose weight, it's not really working very well. I'm doing nothing but yawning. I hate mornings. Garfield got it right completely."***

I sometimes get asked why I am doing what I am doing. Most of the time I can provide a solid, well-reasoned answer. When I first wake up however I find I am invariably asking myself the same question, but then I struggle to find that answer.

I find myself wondering how long I am going to be doing this for. Always waking at the crack of dawn, working all day and then going to bed finally long after the sun has set. I will be doing it for as long as it is necessary. That is the best I can say. I can't fix an end date to this situation. I can't say that a month from now, or six months, or a year it will all be done and I can finally have a lie in without having to worry about what three other people need from me. And that uncertainty is one of the things that makes this situation so challenging mentally. Potentially I could be doing this for the next five years, ten years, or even longer.

06:40am

> ***" My son has decided that my day needs to start now, he needs attention, he's screaming his head off for no reason other than he's awake and no-one is with him. And, of course, going up to see him means that Mum hears everything that is going on so she's now moaning. So my attempt today at getting some me time before the day starts is gone. And if that sounds selfish, then yes, it is. But it is selfish with a purpose.***
>
> ***I don't like being faced with people first thing in a morning, any people. I need time to wake up and start the day myself. When I don't get it, I'm angry, and I'm angry all day long. So I'm not allowed it today so I'm pissed off.***
>
> ***I've got to face mum whinging at me about how she hurts everywhere. I've got to face my son demanding that I play with him. And I am in no mood for either of them now, because neither of them have allowed me to start the day my way."***

God, I really am quite a bitch aren't I? I've said it before and I will say it many more times before I die (and possibly a few more times before I finish this book), I am not a nice man. I am selfish, no argument there. I want what I want and there are still times when I truly resent the situation I am in. It holds me back from doing what I really want to do, from being who I really want to be. Ultimately however I do keep coming back to the fact that I am in this situation through choices I made. I chose to be with my partner, I chose to take care of my mother. These are facts. Having made those choices I cannot and will not desert any one of them. But there are days when that resolve is seriously tested.

07:30am

"The day has started with a vengeance. I took a cup of tea up to mum and some fresh water. She's complaining of nausea and general yuckiness. So I've given her medication, checked her temperature, that's all fine. Of course while I'm doing that my son is clamouring for attention so I got him a bottle of milk and, while I was in with mum, he decided it would be a fun idea to take his nappy off and urinate on the landing through his bedroom gate. Wonderful.

And through all of this my partner slept. So I got her up to deal with my son while I was dealing with my mum. I was probably not very pleasant about the way I woke her up, but at the end of the day, there's a limit to what people can expect of me in terms of social niceties.

So everyone is up, my partner is keeping my son amused. I've done the washing up this morning. The day has well and truly started and the list of jobs is racking up already. I need to phone the doctor today and get them to authorise B12 injections for my mum. I need to phone the district nurses today and get them to sort out night bags for my mum because we only have one left. I've got a mass of shopping I need to get done if I'm going to have everything I need in food-wise for Christmas. It's seven-thirty in the morning and I'm shattered already and I have

no interest in facing the rest of the day, but I have to. It's got to be done.

So what is the deal with these B12 injections? Well a deficiency of vitamin B12 causes a range of symptoms such as tiredness, lethargy and feeling faint. It is also possible that a sufferer may experience altered taste, loss of appetite and maybe even tinnitus. These problems can be rectified by regular injections of B12 (usually every twelve weeks) and that is exactly what my mother had been getting.

Unfortunately, for reasons I have yet to determine it appears that those injections were stopped at some point during my mothers' stay at the nursing home. This means that before those injections can be re-instated a series of blood tests are required followed by a rebuilding of the B12 levels through a series of three injections provided over a week long period.

The problem we currently face is that this is all happening over the Christmas period when blood testing facilities are closed. Therefore we now have to wait before we can do anything to rectify the problem. Not a happy state of affairs. The net result of this is that all hopes of mum enjoying her Christmas the way I had intended are vanishing fast. Frustrated does not even begin to cover how I feel about this.

07:50am

"Everything is just too loud today. I've been up about two hours today and I feel like I've been up all day already. My brain does not want to switch on. We've got the T.V. on in the living room with all kinds of loud and brash kids programmes. My son is sitting there with his little tablet merrily navigating through hordes and hordes of loud and brash nursery rhymes. The noise conflict is driving me slowly insane. I hate mornings and whoever invented mornings I would cheerfully strangle right now.

Are you getting the impression that I am really not a fan of mornings?

This theme may get a little repetitive as this book progresses so I apologise in advance for that eventuality.

My son and his tablet is a constant source of amazement for me. He is only five years old, his communication and motor skills are below what one would expect for a child his age but never make the mistake of thinking this boy is slow or stupid in any way, he absolutely is not. He navigates his way around the functions of that tablet like a true computer pro. Somehow he managed to change the background artwork in favour of a "Spider-man 2" theme which he absolutely loves, God only knows where he found it. And the nursery rhymes he found himself on "youtube". It's fascinating to watch him in action.

08:20am

> ***"The girls have arrived to get Mum ready to face the day. She's going to have another day of bed rest so I've given the girls all their instructions, clued them in on what's going on.***
>
> ***I've got a lot of faith in this team actually. The lead girl is really switched on and all of them are coming across as very caring individuals that are trying to do their best by Mum. It's one of the first times I've been reasonably confident and happy with a team I've been involved with, which is nice. It's one less thing to worry about.***
>
> ***Once they finish up getting Mum ready, then I can give her breakfast to her, along with a fresh cup of tea. Then we'll see how the day progresses."***

One would expect that the Care Team employed to take care of Mums' personal care would require little to no involvement from myself. One would be wrong. My experience of the past three years has shown me that the level of training these girls receive is very low. With my mother suffering relatively complex issues associated with her stroke, without the proper guidance the girls would initially be well out of their depth.

This has been a common theme over the course of the past three years. While the individual carers themselves have, for the most part, proven to be wonderful and caring individuals, they are rarely supported with adequate training and good working practices from the company that employs them.

This is one of the areas where my knowledge base regarding my mothers' condition has proven invaluable. I spend a lot of time co-ordinating with the girls regarding various aspects of my mothers' care, even to the point of providing instruction on how to use the various items of equipment such as the track hoist, slings and the wheelchair.

Technically speaking, this is not my job, however, the girls need to be trained by someone if they are to do the job correctly and to the standard they wish to do it. I often wonder however, how other people manage who do not have someone with them with my knowledge base, understanding and drive.

11.00am

" Everyone's up, everyone's downstairs, my son has turned the living room into a bomb site with his books and toys. I've been out to the shops to get essentials for Christmas, food essentials. I've phoned the Doctors, I've phoned the district nurses, I'm waiting for them both to get back to me on various issues. I've got back, I've had two mouthfuls of a cup of tea and I've prepared the evening meal for tonight which is a slow cooked chicken stew/casserole...... thingy. So everything is chopped up, prepped, in the slow cooker bubbling away, it'll cook all afternoon. Hopefully this means I can get an hour to myself this afternoon. Mum is likely to go back to bed after lunch when the girls come at lunchtime. So maybe I can get an hours peace but I'm not going to hold my breath today.

I have been a bit concerned that my son might be backing up and getting a bit constipated, but since he's merrily

exploding into his nappy, and out of his nappy, that concern seems to have been put to rest at the moment.

In terms of my mothers' activities, today would be classed as a typical day for her. We have a very specialised wheelchair for my mother which provides far more support and extra functionality compared to a standard one. The idea is that with this wheelchair Mum is able to spend far more time out of bed and downstairs with the rest of the family. Under normal circumstances the Care Team will hoist mum into the wheelchair during their morning visit and bring her downstairs. Mum then has the option of spending a half day or a full day downstairs depending on how tired she feels. The girls will then put mum back to bed during either the afternoon or evening visit.

Constipation can be a common element connected to Myotonic Dystrophy and this has certainly been the case where our son is concerned. This is caused because the muscles within the small bowel don't function the way they should. Coupled with the fact that our son is (as has already been noted) an incredibly picky eater this can cause some serious issues, not to mention a great deal of pain and distress. He receives a daily laxative dose in order to help with this, but very close monitoring is also required in order to keep everything operating smoothly.

12:00pm

"Mum's had her lunch now, what we call a fried egg sandwich, basically a lightly fried egg on a round of bread cut into squares, buttered with some brown sauce and salt. She likes her eggs done a particular way and, according to her I am the only one that can get them right. I suppose I'm doing something right at least.

I'd asked my partner to do a couple of jobs this morning when she first got up. I asked her to take some laundry upstairs and put it away. Come midday it's still sitting in the kitchen so I've done it myself. She hasn't even got

dressed yet. My son is kicking up a fuss because he's bored which I completely understand.

Holidays are going to be the most challenging time for us with everyone in the house twenty four-seven. I've asked my partner to get herself dressed and take him out for a walk while we've got something that's reasonable weather wise, just to give him some exercise and maybe wear him out a little bit. Whether or not she does is a different story, we'll see.

I'm rattled today. I'm rattled and really not in the mood. Everything is winding me up. Patience levels right now are at rock bottom, but I keep trying to hold it all together and plug on, what else can I do?

I hate this time of year. But it's the first Christmas in three years that we're going to spend together as a family so I've got to try and make the best of it, especially for my son and my partner as well. Hopefully the day will improve.

Dealing with my partners condition is a real challenge for me. For the most part Myotonic Dystrophy can be classed as a hidden condition (at least for our family), unless you know what to look for there are very few visual symptoms. This makes it very easy to overlook and underestimate its impact. I am well aware that my partner struggles dealing with the impact this condition has on her. She can have bad days where she struggles just to get out of bed, but she can also have good days where she appears relatively "normal". There is no way of predicting day to day how she is going to be feeling.

As for me, Christmas is one of the worst times of year for me. I've never really seen much to celebrate there. I am not religious in the conventional sense so that aspect of the time is meaningless to me and my own memories of previous "celebrations" are not that great. If it wasn't for my son I wouldn't see a reason to bother with it at all.

02:40pm

"I've got some bins now, finally. Obviously with my mothers' needs and my sons' needs I needed higher capacity bins. Unfortunately the local Council are never the quickest organisation on the planet. Six months it's taken, lots of e-mails, lots of complaining, finally two days before Christmas they're delivered. I still don't have a full complement of bins but I have what is essential to the moment. I hate dealing with Government Authorities.

I am very, very tired. My mother has gone back to bed. That was no surprise. I should be hearing something from the district nurses soon regarding mums' catheter. She's having issues with it. It's causing her pain and discomfort. It's a large bore catheter. She's been permanently catheterised for three years now. Pain, discomfort, infections, they are unfortunately part and parcel of dealing with a person who has a permanent catheter fitted. However, I applaud Mum for getting up today, even though it perhaps wasn't the right decision made for the right reasons, she did well.

I wish the same could be said of my partner. I've had to have a conversation with her today. I really don't understand why things are so difficult for her and she can never seem to explain it to me. I ask her questions and all I get as an answer is "I don't know". That's incredibly frustrating. I'm trying to understand, I'm trying to accommodate as best I can. All she seems to want to do is sit on the sofa in her dressing gown with a laptop on her lap and lose herself on-line. I'll never understand how anyone can be content doing that. I go on-line with my games when I get an opportunity to. But for me it's not a

matter of contentment, it's a matter of losing the world for twenty minutes, half an hour, sometimes if I'm really fortunate, an hour. But to stay on there incessantly.

Predictably my son hasn't gone out today, because I've not taken him out. That's how I feel.

I finally designed the front cover for this book. That was a bit of a nightmare, as usual. But, it's done, it's ready.

I've got friends coming around in about half an hour and I can barely keep my eyes open. I hate Christmas.

It doesn't take a rocket scientist to work out that my partner and myself are cut from very, very different cloth. I have a lot of drive, ambition, energy (although that is running a major deficit these days) and determination. I don't like sitting still. I don't like doing nothing. I have to be busy, working, productive. My partner on the other hand does not appear to have any of that, and I just don't get it.

It is, without a doubt, the single largest cause of my frustrations. I want to make her happy. I want her to feel safe and secure. And, above all, I want her to have as many opportunities to explore life as I can provide. None of this, however, seems important to her. If I let it, it could easily drive me to distraction however, I am slowly coming to the conclusion that there is little I can do to change that aspect of her personality so, while I may not like it, while it may (and indeed frequently does) frustrate me, I have to learn to accept it and live with it.

03:30pm

"The District Nurses have just been and gone. They've checked out mums catheter and brought us some more night bags to tide us through until the actual order arrives. They're planning, between Christmas and New Year, to do some blood tests and chase up with the G.P. about the B12 injections for mum. Regarding the catheter, it seems the

catheter itself wasn't the problem. She's getting some quite severe chaffing so we've got barrier cream and a wash to use to try and reduce that and make mum a bit more comfortable, and hopefully that's going to have the desired result.

I can only imagine how uncomfortable it must be to be permanently catheterised. Essentially you have a foreign object permanently fitted into your bladder. There are no end of problems associated with this, the most obvious being the risk of infection. The dangers of this cannot be over-estimated. In a healthy person infections do not necessarily equate to a life threatening condition. In someone who already has a compromised system however, any kind of infection can rapidly evolve into something disastrous. It is an aspect of my mothers' care that I have learnt a lot about over the past three years and I do not take any chances. The moment I feel something is not right I get the professionals out to deal with it before it becomes a major issue.

04:35pm

"We've had a Tesco delivery, more potatoes. I think we've got three, maybe four kilos of potatoes, so we aren't going to run out of them in a hurry.

I've done the washing up, taken mum a cup of tea up. She's looking a lot more comfortable now the District Nurses have been.

Now I'm just waiting for my friends to turn up, spend a bit of time with them, then me and my partner can have tea.

Today has been an impossibly long day. I would have loved to have had a rest part way through but it has just not been possible."

The advent of on-line shopping has been an absolute boon for people such as myself. For someone with such advanced and, at times, complex needs a simple trip to the shops can invariably prove impossible. It takes a lot of organising to provide alternative care in order to leave the house for an extended period. For an hour here and there it's not such a big problem, for the most part, my partner is able to watch over Mum. But for anything more a trained professional is required to take my place. This means that the general weekly shopping trip is effectively out. I can pop out to the local shop for emergency supplies but that is it. Online grocery shopping therefore becomes an incredibly useful tool in the carers arsenal.

06:05pm

> ***"Mum's been fed, unfortunately myself and my partner haven't yet had our tea. Everything has kind of happened at once.***
>
> ***My friends have visited with their two twin girls and that's been a bit of a boost for me. They're a very special family and they mean a lot to me and, in a strange way, their approval of me and what I do means more to me than my own family. They're more like family than friends. I love them to pieces. I love seeing them. I love the fact that they're happy and enjoying life with their girls. I love the fact that they want to share that with me. The two of them have helped me through a lot over the years, probably more than they realise and, if I've become anything of a better person over the years then a large portion of it is down to their help, support, love and affection, and more than a little bit of guidance.***
>
> ***But they've had to get home now. It's time to get their girls to bed. Me and my partner have decided that, since there is only an hour now before our son goes to bed we're going to hold off on having our tea until after he's gone to bed and then maybe, maybe we can relax and eat in peace.***

We'll see if the day ends better than it started. So far the latter half of the day has been far better than the first part, but I am well and truly shattered. I've got a banging in my head now. There's a little pressure building behind my eyes. I can see myself taking some more Ibuprofen tonight. Keep the Migraines at bay, as they say."

I have very clear definitions regarding the concepts of Friends and Family. For me the terms family and relatives are not automatically interchangeable. A relative is someone who you have a connection to through blood only. In my world this connection does not automatically confer love, compassion, understanding or respect. All of those things are earned.

I have only three blood relatives who have also earned the classification of Family, they are, my Daughter, my Son and my Mother. But I do have a small number of people who I have met over the years who I class also as Family. The people I met today are a part of that number.

09:10pm

"The Carers have been and gone and Mum's been settled down with a cup of tea and a mince pie to finish the night off for her. I've just been up to check on her again. She's happily watching T.V. and she'll probably watch that until she falls asleep. I'll check on her again in another hour or so and if need be, turn the T.V. off.

I've had my tea at eight o'clock and I've finally started to feel like the day is drawing to a close. In the end the day ended better than it began. I've managed to avoid getting a headache, which is always good. I can settle down now and watch a film with my partner. Then she'll probably go to bed while I stay up for another couple of hours, do some personal stuff, do some writing. See if I can get to bed before midnight."

As a writer, my biggest challenge is finding time in which to work and, once found, having the energy to make use of that time effectively.

As a rule, by ten o'clock at night the rest of the family are in bed. This means that I have something like a two hour window where I am on my own and way too wired to sleep. Usually I will use this time in one of two ways dependent upon my mood at the time. Either I will play one of my on-line games for a little while or I will try and do some work.

My biggest personal fear is that my role of caring may cause me to lose my career. I don't want to be in a position when this is all over where I have nothing left of my career to go back to. In order to stop that from happening I am doing everything I can now to keep things ticking over, but this added pressure and work load adds at least a couple of hours to every day. Unfortunately, needs must, as the saying goes.

10:20pm

> ***"My partner's just gone to bed. I'm going to go up in a few minutes and turn my mothers' T.V. off and then, at that point, the day is officially done.***
>
> ***I can't go to bed yet, it's too early so I'm going to take some "me" time and do a bit of work. I'll probably end up in bed around midnight I'd guess. I'll try not to be too much later than that.***
>
> ***My partner's just come up to me and gone "Brace yourself, tomorrow's Christmas Eve.". My first instinctive response was, "and?". Christmas doesn't mean anything to me, not really. I will go through the motions for my son. He deserves that at least. But, to be honest, Christmas Eve, Christmas Day, it's just an increased work load as far as I am concerned. Do I feel excited about it? No. But then, I don't really feel excited about anything anymore. Sometimes I wonder where my life went.***

The past three years since my mothers' stroke have been particularly challenging for me. In order to deal with the situation effectively I was forced to remove the emotional content completely. This meant that, to a large extent, I shut down emotionally. The changes to my mother were profound, so much so that, in a very real sense, the person I am now caring for is not the same person I once knew. My mother, as I remember her, is gone. I am not in a position where I can afford the time to grieve for this loss as there is still so much that needs to be done and I am still the only person available to do it. Therefore, in order to remain focussed on the tasks at hand I have had to lock all of those elements of my psyche away. Unfortunately this is not a surgical procedure. I can't just take this element of emotion away and leave the rest in place. Either I lock it all away or none at all.

This has had a knock on effect on every other aspect of my life. All of those gentler emotions, love, compassion, pain, grief, they are all locked away, muted effectively. The only emotion that features prominently in my make-up now is anger although, for the most part, I keep a reasonably good control on that one. I am able to take very little joy or pleasure in anything anymore and I certainly never feel excited about anything.

Day 3

24th December 2014 – Christmas Eve

06:15am

"My alarm went off at six o'clock as always and I was greeted to the dulcet tones of my son. He wasn't being bad or anything, he wasn't even crying for attention, he was just playing. He does that a lot. He talks to himself and plays, and it's quite endearing in its way. But it's still too early, so I asked him to go back to bed, which he did. I turned his light off and told him to go back to sleep for an hour, which he has.

I haven't heard a sound from Mum yet, which I'm not going to object to. I'll be happy if she sleeps through until I wake her up at seven.

I've got a fair few aches and pains this morning, back, neck, shoulders, nothing seems to want to start the day today, but they'll ease off as the day goes on.

Checking my e-mails put a little smile on my face this morning. I got one from Amazon. "How do you like your ladies' nightdress?". If anyone went through and started

reading my e-mails, they'd think I was a very warped individual, and they probably wouldn't be too far wrong but, it just made me giggle.

You see, I do most of my shopping on-line now, I'd say at least ninety to ninety-five percent. Obviously lately I've been buying an awful lot for mum.

Well, it's a much quieter start than yesterday, which is how I like to start the day when I get the chance. Peace, quiet, time to think, time to switch my brain on."

Despite potential evidence to the contrary I am not really some weird recluse with a fetish for old ladies clothing (among other things), honest.

It is one of those elements of caring for Mum that I had never really considered until the first time I was faced with it. Buying new clothing. Mum can't exactly just pop into the local H&M so it falls to me to keep her essential clothing supplies catered for. So far this year I have purchased items such as bras, knickers, nighties and jogging bottoms and, perhaps the most important of all, bed socks.

I won't pretend that it is something I am entirely comfortable doing but, pragmatist that I am, I recognise that it is essential. Woe betide me however, should I fail to get the correct sizes, especially in undergarments. It's one thing to guess wrong with your girlfriend or wife. It's quite another to guess wrong with your own mother.

07:30am

"Mum's awake, she's had her medication, a cup of tea and we've had a little chat about what the plan was for today. With everything that's been going on this week Mum's still feeling a bit fragile so I suggested she just stay in bed today and rest up, conserve her strength so hopefully tomorrow she can spend as much of the day with the

family as possible. She thought this made sense so that's the plan for the day where my mother is concerned.

As for my son, the moment he heard me go upstairs to my mum his door opened. He wanted his attention, but he was good about it. Unfortunately he's decided at some point during the night to take his nappy off and he's wet the bed. Hey ho. The joys of having a five year old with Myotonic Dystrophy.

So, I had to strip his bed this morning and I've got a lot of washing on now, a lot of laundry. So that's all on at the moment. I'll get that dried then I can get his bed made this afternoon.

He was in a good mood though. He came straight in and said hello to Nana, held her hand a bit, pointed out the T.V. again. I think he's got used to the fact that the controls for Nanas' T.V. are out of his bounds.

But we've come downstairs. He's had his obligatory bottle of milk and the T.V.'s on for him and he's got his tablet so he's a happy boy.

And my partner is still asleep.

We've had some concerns over the past couple of months that our son may be showing signs of Diabetes. It is something which is fairly common to sufferers of Myotonic Dystrophy and that, coupled with the fact that I also have Type II Diabetes would mean this would not come as a big surprise. Basically his fluid intake and output have both climbed markedly, especially at night. It may be one of the things that prompts him to wake in the early hours as he invariably asks for a bottle of milk whenever one of us goes in to him.

It is something we are going to have to get checked out once the Christmas holidays are done with.

This is the problem with Myotonic Dystrophy. It is a condition which progresses as the person gets older. New symptoms can appear while, at the same time, existing symptoms can increase in severity. This makes it a constant challenge monitoring the gradual progression of our son and dealing with each new development as it occurs.

09:20am

"A very relaxing half hour. The Carers have been and gone. They've got Mum settled. She's awake and nicely freshened up, ready to face the day. I've given her breakfast and a cup of tea. She's happily chowing down and watching "Miss Marple". She seems quite content at the moment, which is always good.

I've spent the past half hour nicely snuggled up on the couch with my son. He was playing on his tablet, cuddling up to me. He's quite content, he's been very good this morning actually.

I've got the laundry into the drier, meat defrosting, ready for tomorrow and just brought the bins back in. We had a cardboard collection today. So everything is pretty much on track at the moment.

My partner is still in bed. I wonder, if left to her own devices, what time she'd wake up today? Well, as long as my son is being good I'm quite happy to let things continue as they are.

10:30am

"I've taken Mum another cup of tea up. We've had a little bit of a chat about today and tomorrow, what the plan is. Then I decided, twenty past ten, yes, that's a good time to get my partner up otherwise she'll sleep the day away. She won't like that either so, I gave her a gentle knock,

made her a cup of tea and she's now downstairs playing with our son.

This is definitely, at the moment, one of the more relaxed days. So I'm going to do something I don't often do during the day. I'm going to take half an hour, forty minutes for myself, and sit down with one of my games. In fairness, I've been on the run for four and a half hours already so, I think I've earned the right."

I have mentioned my games previously. They are an important aspect of my life. They allow me to disappear from the real world for a brief time allowing me to mentally recharge a little bit. However, as much as I recognise the importance of this I still find myself feeling guilty when I do take the time for them. Intellectually I know this is stupid and I have nothing to feel guilty about but that doesn't alter the feelings I have. It is almost as if I am abandoning my family when I play my games. This is one of those internal battles that I will never completely win, so I no longer try to. I simply accept that these games are necessary for my mental well-being and inject a little bit of rational selfishness into the moment and just, get on with it. There is nothing quite like the human brains capacity to tie itself in intellectual and emotional knots.

11:40am

"I've just given Mum her noon-time medication, taken up her lunch to her. She seems quite settled and happy. Everything is still quite calm and relaxed. I'm waiting for the bomb to drop almost.

Having said that, I've just had a nice discussion with my partner regarding our son and the state of his nails. He is developing a lovely set of jet black talons that need cutting. Both fingers and toes. And he is not going to like that one little bit. For some reason he hates having them done and he screams like we're killing him. So we're trying to work out when the best time to do that is, and,

ultimately there is no best time, you just pick a time and do it.

And I am looking forward to that like the proverbial hole in the head. Hey ho."

What is it about children that makes them kick up such a fuss over the simplest of tasks? I don't think it is ever going to be something that I can understand. What I do know is that it is incredibly frustrating. Something that should take a matter of a few minutes of concentrated effort devolves rapidly into a nightmare of tears, screaming and tantrums ;lasting easily in excess of half an hour or even an hour. By the end of the whole process my partner and I are both physically and mentally drained and deaf as posts.

At least we know what's going on. God only knows what the neighbours may be thinking when we are doing this.

01:00pm

"The Carers have been, freshened Mum up a bit for the afternoon and Mum's decided she's going to have a bit of a kip so, as I am ahead of the game today, which is an unusual occurrence, I'm going to follow suit. I am absolutely shattered so I'm going to put my head down for a couple of hours.

My partner and my son are merrily playing away. I've got all of the washing out of the drier and folded. Time to close my eyes.

I am a little bit concerned at the moment though with the Care Staff. We seem to be going through an awful lot of them in a short space of time. We've seen four different faces in the past two days and that is quite a lot. I'm hoping this is just a glitch over the Christmas period but it

is something I will monitor very closely. We'll see how we go."

I have had mixed experiences with Care Agencies over the past three years. As a general commentary my experiences have taught me that the girls themselves tend to be very nice people. With only a small number of exceptions they tend to be very caring individuals who genuinely want to do their best for the client. What I have found is that they tend to be very poorly supported by the management side of the operation.

There are two main failings in the management of a care agency based on what I have seen so far. The first is in the training provided. The level of training the girls have received varies considerably. Part of the problem I believe is that the legal requirements in this regard are simply too low. There are people working in this industry that have only the vaguest concept of how to use hoist equipment correctly and their basic knowledge of proper moving and handling techniques is well below what is required. This is not the fault of the girls themselves, rather the blame lies primarily with the Government. The "standards" imposed by legislation are so impossibly low a carer can virtual be brought straight of the street and put directly to work. The Agencies have no incentive to train their staff any further than is legally required because that costs them money. This contributes directly to the general dissatisfaction of the Care Staff and, in turn, the high turnover of Staff within a company. The knock on effect of that on the client is the virtual absence of continuity of care.

I have personally faced situations in the past where the turnover has been so high within the Agency employed to care for my mother that I no longer made any attempt to remember names of individuals and I had lost all confidence in the staff arriving each day.

The Care Profession deals with individuals at their most vulnerable. Continuity of care should be paramount, unfortunately, my experience shows this to be the exception rather than the rule.

04:00pm

"I got up at three as I said. I'm feeling a bit more refreshed, how long for, I do not know. I checked in with Mum, but she was sound asleep so I left her to it. I'm just about to go up and check on her again. I'll make her a cup of tea and wake her up this time. I'll give her the evening medication than come down and cook tonight's evening meal.

It doesn't look like I was the only one in the house sleeping. I came down and my son was fast asleep on the carpet, wrapped in a blanket with a bottle in his mouth, looking adorable as always. And my partner had done the washing up which was really gratifying.

Yeh, today's a good day."

One of the most prominent effects of my mothers' stroke has been the lasting fatigue. It really doesn't take much to wear my mother out anymore. This makes it really challenging trying to find ways to provide a good quality of life for her and allow her to try and do some of the things she used to do and would like to do again. Things like painting, embroidery, writing. I'm hoping that over time we can improve the situation and that with a little help and some directed Physiotherapy Mum will regain some of her strength. I guess this is something only time will tell.

Mum however, is not the only one who suffers with excessive fatigue. It is also a common symptom associated with Myotonic Dystrophy which means both my partner and my son are affected by it. As a rule my son will have a nap at least once a day. It's just the times that vary and of course this is also affected by how active he has been during the day., I know he is my son, and I am biased but I have to say, when he is asleep he is the cutest little boy on the planet. This of course might have something to do with the fact that he is not destroying anything and there is an air of peace and quiet.

05:20pm

"We've all been fed. I've kept things simple tonight, I've done a kind of Bolognaise but with Tuna instead of mince. It's a dish I've done before. It's nice and quick and easy, very filling with lots of vegetables in it and, surprisingly, my son even had some. He liked it so much he had three bowls, two of which came off my plate. I'm very impressed, very happy with him. I always love it when he enjoys his food and eats a lot because I worry about what he eats all the time. So that's been a result today.

There was still a portion of stew left from yesterday so I've put that into a container, labelled it up and it's gone into the freezer. That's a portion of food for another day, probably for me on a day when I'm not feeling so good, or something like that. But I loathe and detest throwing good food away. It'll keep for a couple of weeks in the freezer. I can re-heat it in the microwave, nice and easy.

Now I'll check on Mum, have a cup of tea. Mum's been feeling a bit drowsy this afternoon so I'm not sure that she's going to have eaten a lot.

We've had the delivery while I was asleep, for mum, all of the supplies she needs to maintain the catheter, so that's about a months' worth of supplies there. It's like having a prescription, I have to keep renewing it and get new deliveries in. At least we've got that ball rolling now and I've got all the details I need to be able to renew myself in future, so that's good.

It constantly amazes me, the amount of material that is required in order to look after Mum. There are so many things I have to monitor and keep in stock. That's a job all in itself. There is obviously the supplies necessary for Mums catheter which itself is changed every twelve weeks or so. The leg bag that attaches to the catheter needs replacing weekly, then there is the larger capacity night bag which needs to be replaced daily. Then there's my mothers' medication for which I get a months supply at a time. Then the general supplies concerned with mums' personal care, bed mats, Tenna pads, baby wipes and various toiletries, creams and the like. It would be very easy to lose track of all of these things if you're not careful. So I guess it's a good job that I am.

07:15pm

"The girls are here to put mum to bed, well, she's already in bed so they'll clean her up, change her nightie, settle her back down again and generally make her feel relaxed and fit. Then I'll go up with a cup of tea and a mince pie and give her her medication and settle her down for the night.

Then I think me and my partner will settle down with some stuff, watch something on the telly and see how things go.

09:00pm

"I've just watched "The Flash" with my partner, now I'm going to go up and check on Mum, see if she's finished her mince pie and her cup of tea, then get her settled down for the night. She's probably already asleep by now.

Then back down here. Watch something else with my partner and then finish off my nights work which is washing up and prepping for tomorrows festivities.

I think tomorrow is going to be quite stressful. I'm expecting the two Carers who are coming in tomorrow to be people who have never been here before. If that's the case then I'm not going to be very happy because that means that all of my attention is going to be diverted to training them on what they have to do, which is not going to put me in a good mood. But we shall see.

I am one of those peoples who lives by their plans, and that level of organisation is essential to the way are lives are currently led. I don't react well when events work to divert me from a prepared plan of action, especially when I feel those events could have been avoided. I pride myself on my organisational skills. It is just unfortunate that my patience levels are not equal to those skills. Ultimately though, this causes more problems for other people than it does for me.

11:05pm

> ***"My partner's been in bed for nearly an hour, I sent her off there knowing that we've got an early start tomorrow and she's going to need her sleep.***
>
> ***I've still got the washing up to do and I've still got the prep for tomorrow. I've had a lazy hour just doing stuff on the computer, getting my head together.***
>
> ***I think the thing I struggle most with is the bi-polar. It makes it very difficult for me to focus on tasks and stay on point. It's not a natural thing for me anymore. I prize my me time. Being around people as much as I am these days is a challenge. I am not a natural people person, not by any stretch of the imagination.***
>
> ***A part of me is dreading tomorrow. I've got three people who I want to have a good time, as good as I can make it, which means I've got to keep my head together, keep focussed, not get stressed. I need to stay in the background and keep things running for them, and I don't know if I can do that. It is a challenge, but, somehow I'll find a way through.***

Everyone wears masks. Everyone has elements of their personality or psyche they don't want others to see. I just do it more than most. I spent a long time trying to understand myself and trying to deal with the depressive states that can, at times, threaten to overwhelm me. I wear masks constantly to hide this aspect of my personality from those around me. They need to see a happy man, in control, strong and capable. Whether that is what I am feeling or not is totally irrelevant. Their security is drawn from my strength and ability to keep control of our surroundings and I cannot let that image slip. Not ever.

12:25am

> ***"The washing up's done and I'm about as prepped as I'm ever going to get for tomorrow, and I know I should be going to bed now, but I am so wired.***
>
> ***If I went to bed now I would just toss and turn. There's no point, my brain just won't shut down. My whole body feels like it's waiting, waiting for something to happen.***
>
> ***I'm not excited about tomorrow, I'm dreading it. I just want it to be done, dusted and over. I've said it before and I'll say it again, I make Scrooge look like a Saint. I hate Christmas. It is stressful, it is irritating, it is expensive and I just do not see the point. But if it puts a smile on my little man's face then I guess that is the point. Here's hoping. Here's hoping tomorrow doesn't turn into one long nightmare.***
>
> ***I'm going to sit down now and try and watch something, try and tire my mind out. The odds are pretty good that I'm going to end up sleeping down on the sofa tonight. If I try to go to bed I'll just end up keeping my partner awake by tossing around."***

Sleep has always been a rare and valued commodity for me. I have struggled with insomnia as far back as I can remember. Under normal circumstances this would not pose much of a problem. However, as you have probably worked out by now (and if you haven't, what have you been reading?), I do not live in normal circumstances.

I am on the go eighteen hours a day on average, seven days a week. This is not a routine or pace that I can maintain without decent sleep. Maybe someone should tell my Insomnia that. I won't medicate myself to sleep. What would happen if I was in a drugged up slumber and a member of my family had an emergency during the night? No, that's too risky an option to even consider. If there is a way to settle my mind then I have yet to find it. I really hope that changes sometime soon though.

Day 4

25th December 2014 – Christmas Day.

07:20am

"Merry Christmas. Yeh, right. It was after four before I managed to get to sleep. Even then I tossed and turned. I slept on the couch, didn't bother going upstairs. For reasons best known to someone else my alarm didn't go off and, if my partners did, she didn't move to it, so it was just after seven before I actually got up. So I'm now running on three hours. I have had no time to myself. I've got straight up, made cups of tea for Mum, taken that up to her, given her her medication, got the little one out of bed, well, he got himself out of bed, he was already up. I brought him downstairs, changed him, got his milk, got his breakfast and now I'm having the first cigarette of the day and the first cup of tea.

The whole plan for today has been shot to pieces. The first thing I get when I walk into Mum is, "I'm not feeling well, I think I'll stay in bed all day." Great. She may as well have stayed at the nursing home. The most important day of the year for everyone else and she's going to stay in bed. I give up.

So I guess my partner, son and mother will sort Christmas presents out in their own time. Me, I'll just slave away in the kitchen all day and be done with it. This day cannot pass fast enough for me already. I want it over, I've already got a headache and I haven't even been up half an hour yet. I'm in a bad mood. I'm irritable and I fucking hate Christmas."

Even I'm cringing a little as I write this. But let's be honest. I've said all along that I am not a nice guy. I wasn't joking. This book was never going to paint me in a favourable light, at least, not if I was going to be honest about things.

I get frustrated easily, that's a fact. When I am already tired it is so much worse. We all have a vision in our heads of what Christmas Morning is supposed to be like and this was so far removed from that vision it just wasn't even funny. I wanted everyone to be happy and smiling. I wanted to feel their excitement and pleasure. But none of that happened. I felt like everything I had done and was still doing was utterly worthless.

08:30am

"My partner is still in bed. The Carers have arrived. I hope they know what they're doing. Mum's staying in bed so it shouldn't be too complicated, not too much moving around for her.

I checked her temperature. That's fine, but she is still complaining of the odd spasm and being drowsy. I think it's this lack of B12. That's the most obvious cause to my mind.

My son is happy enough, playing on his tablet. He's been giving me lots of hugs this morning, that's always nice.

So far it's pretty much like any other day. I've got the meat out ready to start roasting and I've started sorting through the vegies. That's it really."

There is never a good time to start playing nurse to the person you are caring for but, you can guarantee, if there is a time that is really inopportune then that is exactly the time when things will choose to happen.

Over the past three years I have become pretty good at recognising and, to a point, diagnosing symptoms where my mother is concerned. I know what to look for and, more importantly I know what information is going to be needed when I have to start calling in the professionals. This makes the whole process a lot quicker and easier when that point is reached.

The thing is my mothers' entire system is compromised as a result of the stroke. She is wide open to infections of all sorts and they can rapidly progress into something potentially life threatening if left unattended for too long.

It doesn't matter what day or time of year it is, for me the rules are still the same. There are signs I am constantly on the lookout for. Temperature, skin colour and condition, cognitive function, pain symptoms outside of the day to day norms. Any one of these could be an indicator of something serious going on. It is part of my job description to be aware of it and, if I can, to stop it.

09:45am

"The weather is as cheery as I feel, it's throwing it down outside, it's grey, overcast, it's horrible. What is it about Christmas? Why can I never get in the mood for it?

My partner has finally got up. Mum's been fed. The carers are gone. My son is ok, he just wants attention and I'm not in the mood. My Bi-polar coupled with fatigue and

general malaise. I don't like this time of year. I can't understand what everyone finds so exciting about it. I just want it to be over. I'm expected to be happy and cheerful, how can I be happy and cheerful? I don't know. I don't know happy and cheerful, it's not a natural state for me. It's always forced. Hey ho, I'll just keep trucking on."

It is the nature of life that, when you make a choice over one element of your life one of the results of that decision is the removal of options or choices from other aspects of your life. Such is the case here.

I made the choice to care for my mother and to create this somewhat unusual family structure. That means the choice over whether or not to celebrate Christmas is removed for me. It is at times like these that I start to feel resentment. In part, this is aimed at the people around me. A much larger portion however is aimed at the world and life in general. I feel like everything is conspiring to force me into the position I now find myself.

I am not deeply religious but I do occasionally give a thought to concepts such as predetermination. At times like this I really start to wonder how much of my life is actually under my control and how much is under the control of some unseen force. A part of me almost wishes there was an outside force dictating from the wings. I quite like this concept as it provides me with someone else to whom I can direct the force of my ire, no matter how unreal they may be.

11:05am

"I've re-worked the entire day so I'm doing the Christmas meal for this evening. With Mum staying in bed there's no point stressing myself trying to get it done for lunch-time so she can eat with us.

She's still very tired and woozy, but she's tried to be involved. We took my son in there, opened the presents. There were a few moments of fun and stuff but I don't

think my son really understands what it's all about either, and it's a difficult concept to communicate. But he opened a couple of presents, handed a couple out and then manifestly got bored and wanted to do other things. That's my son.

I don't know what all the fuss is about at Christmas, I really don't.

But he's back downstairs, happily playing away on his tablet. My partner is on her computer, and I'm just wishing the day away.

I'll do Mum her meal in about half an hour and then I might think about getting something to eat. I've just realised I've not eaten anything yet today."

I should probably clarify some of the Christmas arrangements at this point. In setting things up for today my main objective was to provide as many opportunities to include Mum in the proceedings as possible. Of course this entire thought process pre-supposed that Mum would be using her wheelchair for at least part of the day.

In terms of the Christmas decorations I had elected for a minimal approach downstairs whilst placing the majority, including the tree and Christmas presents in Mums' room. The idea was to generate as much of a happy and celebratory vibe as possible.

I had intended for us to go into Mums' room early and open all the presents around Mum over a cup of tea before the carers arrived. Then we could adjourn downstairs for the rest of the morning with Mum in her wheelchair. We would have had the Christmas meal at lunchtime downstairs and then if Mum wanted to go back to bed after lunch when the Carers came she could do that.

Obviously that entire plan was blown out of the water right from the start so now I was faced with playing catch up and working on the fly.

This was never destined to put me in a happy mood.

12:40pm

"What to say. Mum's had her lunch. She didn't eat all of it. She's still not feeling great. She's complaining of being nauseous and woozy and dizzy. This is that B12. The lack of it's completely knocked her for a loop so this is something we have really got to try and get sorted as soon as this Christmas period is over and we can get blood tests done. But, in the meantime, it's just a case of trying to keep Mum as comfortable as possible, keep the fluid balance up and let her rest when she wants to rest. There's nothing more I can do. She's all apologetic that she is causing me so much trouble, she feel she's spoiled our Christmas because I'm having to focus so much on her and she can't involve herself in it and enjoy it the way she wanted to.

Now this is why I hate times like Christmas. Society expects so much of people at Christmas and I think it is ridiculous. That's what adds the pressure. We're told, "It's Christmas, you have to enjoy. You should be happy and joyous, cheerful and ...", what a load of claptrap. It's another day in the week. Live it the same way as you've lived every other. If you're living them joyful then carry on being joyful, if you're pissed off then be pissed off.

You see, I don't give a crap what society thinks of me. In fact I don't really give a crap what anyone thinks of me.

Anyway, the Carers have been for the afternoon session. Mum's settled down again. We might have an issue of water retention in the legs which is something I'm going to have to monitor quite closely over the next few days. If that seems to develop then it'll be a case of getting the

District nurses and the G.P. out again and getting Mum re-assessed.

I still haven't managed to have anything to eat yet. I think my Brother is going to be phoning soon so I'm going to wait until that happens until I get some food."

As you've probably guessed by now I'm a little bit of a closet Philosopher and I have little patience with the numerous rules and conventions of modern day society. Don't misunderstand, I am no Anarchist. A society needs rules and guidelines it's just that, since the advent of "Political Correctness" Society has been slowly driving itself insane trying to find ways to effectively police peoples thoughts and words in ways that are, frankly absurd. This is something for which I have no time.

And Societies response to events such as Christmas is utterly unfathomable. I've been a grouchy old bastard for three hundred and sixty four days of the year but hey, today is Christmas , put your happy face on. Well, I'm sorry, but my happy face got run over by a truck about the same time I was born. I am a grouchy old bastard and I will remain a grouchy old bastard. That is my right. And if you think I'm bad at Christmas, just wait until I start talking about Birthdays.

04:30pm

"I've served the "Christmas Meal". I took it up to my mum who then told me she was feeling nauseous. I served it to my partner and I was going to serve it to my son but then found that he'd exploded into his nappy and no-one had bothered noticing while I was in the kitchen for two hours. So we've had to change him. Then, when I tried to feed him he decided he didn't want any so that's gone by the board.

The past forty minutes has just been one big stress after another and one big irritation after another. By the end of

it I've got a plate of food sitting there that I've got zero interest in touching. So I've been up since seven o'clock this morning, it's now four-thirty in the afternoon, I still haven't eaten and I'm no longer hungry. Merry Christmas me. Whoever invented this day wants fucking shooting.

And my partner hasn't even got dressed yet. What a fucking day this is. I've just got no interest anymore. So I'll just have this cigarette and then start tidying the kitchen up which looks like a bomb's hit it. I hate being an untidy cook."

Upon reading this you could be forgiven for believing that this is all about me. Oh woe is me, the poor little boy stuck living a life he never wanted. Well, to a point there is an element of that to all of this. I told you, I'm selfish. I wanted some happiness today. The way that was going to happen was by making my family happy yet, it seemed, everything I tried to do in order to accomplish that was failing in a spectacular fashion. My mum was too ill to be involved how she wanted to be, my partner appeared completely disinterested in the whole day. In fact, the only one who seemed in any way content was my son and that was probably because he didn't really understand the importance of the day.

05:05pm

"I've had enough. Why I bother I do not know. I've just spent the past thirty-five minutes cleaning up the kitchen and washing up, at the beginning of which my partner comes in, tells me what a lovely meal I've cooked which I have yet to taste, it's still sitting on the side, untouched. She asks me what I'm doing, I tell her. Her response is "Oh, well I need to sit down. I'm full and I'm happy.". Wonderful. Thanks for the help. Thanks for the assist. Much appreciated.

Having done all the washing up, I go upstairs to find that Mum has barely had four forkfuls of her food. She proclaims it as "tasty", how she would know that I don't know. So, all in all, a complete waste of three hours effort.

Can I just ban Christmas because I am just sick of it?"

My partners powers of observation are a constant amazement to me. There are times, I swear, when a blind zombie would be aware of more going on than she is.

I love the girl to distraction (admittedly that may not be immediately obvious at the moment) and that is exactly why I get so frustrated with her sometimes.

06:30pm

"I've just put our son to bed. He passed out half an hour ago. Just waiting for the girls to come now and get Mum settled down for the night.

I'm really angry about this B12 situation, it's really knocked Mum flat and it has impacted on how she's been able to enjoy the day, and that doesn't please me at all."

I think the main problem with today, with the whole week in fact, is that I had certain expectations.

Let's just back track for a moment and look at the events that brought us to this day.

It has been three years since my Mum had her stroke. For the first two of those I was stuck with my Mum in Scotland. So this year was going to be the first of the three where we would all be together again over the Christmas period. It was what I had been working to achieve for all that time and now it was finally here.

I guess I hoped or expected this day to be almost symbolic of the end of that journey. A true celebration if you like. Yet somehow it didn't work out that way. #

Ultimately I think that was my fault. I'm not trying to be some kind of Martyr here. You see, for the first time in my life I actually felt that I had a Christmas day that was symbolic of something worth celebrating, yet, when it came down to it, I seemed to be the only one interested in doing the celebrating.

Now I am being unfair to the rest of my family here, I realise that. Obviously there was no way I could account for my Mothers' physical state on the day. And while the situation with the B12 was certainly something I feel could have been avoided, my three years of experience tells me categorically that if not that then there may well have been some other issue that occurred to mar my mothers' enjoyment of the day.

As for my partner and son there is an area of their condition that I still struggle to get to grips with. Facial expressions. Myotonic Dystrophy affects the facial muscles and usually results in those muscles not working in the same way as they would in you or I. In practical terms this means that they do not give off the same visual communication cues as other people do. It is only when you are faced with a condition like this that you realise just how much a part of communication facial expression really is.

As I now reflect back on that day and take the time to factor in these elements one thing becomes abundantly clear to me. I had inadvertently allowed Societies perception of what this day should be to feed in to my own expectations. I had effectively created a mental ideal image of the day that none of the three could ever hope to match.

This wasn't so much ,making a rod for my own back, as it was, making a bloody great flag pole and sticking it up my arse. There are times when my level of ineptitude amazes even me.

01:35am

"For someone whose day started at seven, on about three hours sleep, I don't think I'm doing too bad.

My partner has just gone to bed which means I know I'm not going to see her before ten o'clock tomorrow. I'm going to be going to bed soon. I've got to be up at six, seven at the latest.

The day ended better than it started. My partner got me a birthday present for next year. My birthday is in January. She allowed me to open it early because I knew what it was. I was there when she bought it for me. A board-game. "Monopoly", but a special edition version of the "Marvel" comics. It's got some cool quirks to it. So we played that and, predictably, if you play Monopoly with two people it's not going to be a quick game. Ultimately I conceded defeat. It was a bit of fun at the end.

I think my whole issue with today is my expectations of the day. It's been a challenge today. I'm going to go to bed not knowing whether it was a success or not really. I think that the best that can be said is, we survived. But then, I'm coming to realise that's what life's all about. Survival."

Day 5

26th December 2014 – Boxing Day

06:15am

"I'm up. I'm moving. I am really tired. I am going to try and get half an hour to myself before I have to start running around after Mum and my son.

The plan today is to let my partner sleep in as much as possible, but at some point, certainly after lunch, I'm going to be needing a lie down. I know I'll can't make the whole day without rest but we'll see what happens."

Yes, I've started a new day on the back of less than four hours sleep. By anyone's standards that is not a lot. I am one of those fortunate people that can function for ridiculously long periods on very small amounts of sleep. Having said that I am only too well aware that the long term effects are not good.

06:45am

"I've had a chance to wake up. After yesterdays' fiasco I decided to have some breakfast.

I can hear my son upstairs. He's ready to get up. So, it's time to make Mum a cup of tea and take that up, give her

her pills and everything and then get the little lamb up. Then the chaos begins again for another day."

07:30am

"Mum's up. She's a little bit chipper than yesterday. I don't think I'll be recommending that she gets out of bed, but I'll leave the decision up to her. She's had her medicine, a cup of tea, she's sat now watching the T.V. while we wait for the girls to arrive. She's had a glass of milk today, odd one that.

My son meanwhile, has left me lots of fun and games. He's taken his nappy off again and wet the bed. So I've had to strip the bed this morning, get that into the washing machine. That's another load of washing I've put on. Get my son changed, dressed, settled down with his tablet and the T.V., and a bottle of milk. He's happy. He's a good little lad really.

In many ways there's lots of similarities between my son and mum. They're both at opposite ends of the spectrum but I have communication issues on both sides. I don't understand either of them sometimes, and that is the root of a lot of my frustrations."

Basic communication with both my mother and my son can be extremely challenging. There is so much I have to constantly remember which lies outside the normal parameters.

In my mothers' case there are the difficulties with her short term memory. I can often find myself going over the same conversation time after time during the course of any given day. I find this experience very surreal, it's like I'm playing a role in "Groundhog Day". It is also very frustrating as I am not given to repeating myself under normal circumstances. Add to that my mothers' perception of the passage of time, which is virtually non-existent, and things can get very interesting, very quickly, and not in a good way.

09:00am

> ***"The Carers have been and gone. Mum is generally a lot brighter than yesterday, which is good. She's sitting up in bed with her breakfast, a cup of tea and watching the "Strictly Christmas Special". That was a big, big boon, getting Sky Multi-room in this place. Knowing how mum can fall asleep at the drop of a hat I felt that the ability to record shows and play them back later, pause shows part way through, all of these sorts of things, and just the sheer variety that's on offer was really going to benefit Mum. And that's paying dividends which is nice.***
>
> ***The washing is in the drier now. I should have that folded and ready to go back upstairs soon.***
>
> ***My son is still quite content so I'm going to crack on and get the evening meal prepped. I'm going to use up some of yesterdays' beef joint. I'll chop it up and make a beef stew. Use the slow cooker for it. That's another really useful piece of kit in our situation. I can prep stuff first thing in a morning and let it cook all day long in the slow cooker and we can get some nice, solid, tasty meals with, not a massive amount of effort which is great.***

One of my on-going challenges in setting up the home environment has been trying to work out ways of providing equipment and facilities that will benefit Mum in her current condition. A T.V. in Mums' room was not a great lead of logic, however that alone wouldn't have really given Mum what she needed. To begin with, even with Freeview Mum would not have had access to some of the programmes she likes. Also Mum can fall asleep without warning so with a normal T.V. this would invariably mean she would very rarely see an entire show. Therefore the ability to record shows, especially those showing late at night, and play them back in part or full at a time of Mums' choosing becomes incredibly useful, especially at times like these where Mum is too ill to get out of bed.

Mums condition has left her in a position where a large number of her former pleasures have been denied to her. It is a part of my job description to try and find ways I can give her back some of those pleasures again, at least in part.

10:10am

> ***"I've got tonight's main meal bubbling away. I've checked in on Mum, she's doing fine. I've made her a fresh cup of tea. She's happy watching the tail end of "Strictly" and she says she's probably going to have a little bit of a morning nap until lunch-time which actually isn't that far away now. I've given the kitchen a complete tidy around, cleaned all the surfaces down, hoovered and steam-mopped the floor so that's all nice and fresh. I do like that steam mop actually, but I've taken to spraying a little "Detol" surface cleaner on there first. It freshens the whole thing up a little bit I think. It's quite nice.***
>
> ***I'm just having a quick cigarette. I've played a little bit with my son. I'll go up and get my partner up in a few minutes, make her a cup of tea and then, hopefully I can sit down and chill for an hour before I have to think about making Mums' lunch."***

I know that if some of my friends read this they will be truly amazed at the level of domesticity I am currently exhibiting. It is a strange thing but this is the first house where I have really felt the impulse to try and keep it as clean and tidy as I can. My natural state in all honesty is a little slobbish so believe me when I say this comes as much of a surprise to me as it does anyone else.

I guess that I have invested so much more time energy and emotion into this house than I have any in the past. I have really done everything I can over the past year to try and make this place feel as much of a home as I can for my three charges. The net result of this for me is that I actually feel like this is a family home. I've never felt that before. I really want to look after it and make it work for all of us. I want my family to be happy and comfortable here. Could I finally be settling down at forty-five?

11:50am

"I've had twenty minutes to chill a little bit between tasks. I've just made Mum her lunch, taken that up to her, given her her pills, cup of tea and set her up with the Christmas episode of "Dr. Who". That'll take her through her lunchtime quite happily. Then we can get the girls in, get her settled down for the afternoon. She's probably going to have a kip once the girls have been. There's a good chance I will as well.

I'm going to have a bite to eat now, a couple of rounds of toast and then yeh....job done."

05:00pm

"I've been up for a couple of hours. I got the evening meal finished, served up for everyone apart from the little lamb yet. I'll try him with a bit soon.

Mum's still not feeling brilliant. She's complaining of a change in her sense of taste, so I guess that's something I'm going to have to get checked out when I can get the doctor out. Other than that it's business as usual apart from one major event.

We have snow. We have snowflakes the like of which I've never seen since I was a kid. It's thick, it's big, looks like it's here to stay. Strangely enough it's the first time I've actually felt like this is Christmas. It's amazing what a bit of weather does. We brought my son out to see it and he

was all excited and energised by it. There is something quite magical about seeing snow on the ground. It's nice. We're getting a lot of it though."

So I guess I'm not so much of a Scrooge after all. There is a cleanliness and purity associated with snow that instantly brings on a feeling of peace in me. It brings back some of the few pleasant childhood memories. As a young teenager I could often be seen walking across the local hills when the snow was down. The crunch of the snow, the fresh, crisp taste to the air, and the silence, these are all things I remember with a great deal of pleasure. I miss those times.

06:40pm

"I've just spent twenty minutes on two different phone calls to medical services. I'm concerned about Mum. Her temperature is going a bit silly, up and down like a yo-yo. She's flushed, she's cold and clammy to the touch. Her urine output is very, very low from what I would normally expect and very dark to the point that I'm suspecting there might even be blood in it. None of these are particularly good signs but they are also things that I've come across so often in the past three years.

Obviously, it's Boxing Day, we've just had a wonderfully heavy snow fall so it's the perfect time to try and rally the out-of-hours service. So, I've put a phone call in. I've just got to wait now for the Doctor to phone me back and then we see where we go from there. I would prefer for her to be seen, to be honest. These are the kinds of things I like to try and nail on the head because if you let it develop for too long, it becomes a serious issue and, in my Mums' case, a serious issue usually means Hospital and could potentially mean a lot worse. I'm not going to take that chance now that I've finally got her home. So the next few

hours are going to be devoted to various different medical services and we'll see how we go."

And that's how fast things can change. Over the past three years I have gotten quite used to the rapidity in which Mums' condition can deteriorate. As I've mentioned previously, the fact that Mum is permanently catheterised leaves her prone to Urinary Tract Infections. Add to that Mums' impaired swallow reflex which leaves her at risk of food and fluid aspiration which can cause chest infections. Then factor in the time of year and its associated risks of cold and flu viruses, you can see there's quite a lot to contend with. As Mums' system is already severely compromised as a result of the stroke any one of these can become a very serious issue in a very short space of time.

These are continual, daily risks. The only way to combat them is through constant vigilance on my part. As you can tell from the diary entry I have become fairly adept at determining symptoms and assessing Mums' condition. Due to my knowledge base, that task has proven to be relatively straight forward. The trick however is to observe covertly.

The one thing that the stroke left largely intact with my Mum was her brain. She still retains a lot of the analytical qualities she used to have, the only problem now is that she has a tendency to overthink things and think the worst. My job is to observe her condition in a way that leaves her unaware of my concerns. Were she to register concern or anxiety from me then that would serve as a cue for her to believe the worst possible scenario. In effect she would end up "thinking" herself sicker.

07:40pm

"I've done all the phone calls with the emergency out of hours service and the net result is that I am just waiting for a Doctor to visit. Exactly when that will happen is anybody's guess. In that respect, and referring back to earlier this evening when I was so "joyous" over the snow fall, now, in retrospect, we couldn't have picked a worse

> ***night. The weather conditions, time of the year, that's all going to make things challenging now. I guess we just sit back and wait. Based on the telephone conversation, they're classing it as an urgent case and they're already talking about possible hospitalisation. I've spoken to Mum about this, even though I already knew what her feelings were. They pretty much mirror my own. Wherever possible we are going to avoid Hospital. Whenever Mum goes into Hospital, she comes out worse than she went in. It causes us more problems than it solves. So, we shall see."***

As much as I don't want to be too disparaging of the N.H.S. my experiences of the past three years has shown that the standard of care they provide can be somewhat erratic to say the least.

The problem as I see it is, simply put, they don't know my Mum. She comes on to a ward where no one knows who she is or what the true extent of her issues are and they don't take the time to properly familiarise themselves with the patient during the initial assessment. This leads to inadequate or inappropriate levels of care further down the line. It's all the little things which, when ignored, mount up to a truly uncomfortable experience for my mother.

They never acknowledge that my Mum has complex pain issues. Neuropathic pain coupled with her dislocated shoulder make all moving and handling exercises difficult. Her left sided inattention means that she does not see anything on the left so, when people approach from that side without warning it startles Mum. Also when drinks are placed too far to the left in front of her she cannot see them.

I think my biggest complaint is their attitude towards me. At best I am viewed as an over-involved son who worries too much at worst an outright irritant. I am never viewed as a potential asset. What they rarely consider is the fact that, as Mums primary carer for three years I am perhaps the most experienced person in the room when it comes to the peculiarities of Mums' condition. I am a potentially huge resource which is all too often ignored.

Wherever possible I always work to avoid Mum going into hospital. Mum hates the experience and I always end up spending the first several weeks on her return home recovering her condition to the point it was at prior to the hospital visit.

09:50pm

> ***"Mum's fast asleep. The Doctor's been. He's pronounced everything pretty O.K.. There's nothing really to worry about at this point. No obvious sign of infection. I'll monitor her over the weekend then I'll have to chase things up with Mum's G.P. on Monday.***
>
> ***We've got to get these B12 injections sorted out so that we can get Mum up and out of bed.***
>
> ***So I'm going to chill down now and do a bit of work. I might even end up in bed before midnight with a bit of luck. The first time in three days. I might end up getting more than four hours sleep for once. That would be nice."***

This was the first time using the out of hours service with respect to my mum since I had brought her back to England. I had used it on a number of occasions while Mum was still in Scotland, and to good effect. Following all of the assorted press that the service in England had received over the past year or so I wasn't quite sure what to expect.

In fairness I was pleasantly surprised. The net result could be best described as quick and efficient, that even taking the weather into account. Prior to this event it was an area of my mothers' care with which I had some trepidation. Having experienced the system now in action I felt a lot more comfortable going forward.

11:00pm

"My partner's just gone to bed. I am going to spend an hour winding down on the computer, hit one of my games, switch off. Everyone's in bed and settled. I should get in bed by midnight and, by my standards, that's still pretty early. Six hours sleep for a change. That'll come in handy.

Tomorrow's my partners' birthday. She's worried that I'm recording these things and I'm being unkind to her, that I'm complaining about her. And I guess there will be some of my journal entries here where I'm not overly flattering, but it's the truth. I'm saying things how I see them.

The one thing that's abundantly clear to me is that my partner is no more perfect than I am and I am a long way from perfect. But, despite, or even because of her imperfections I love her. That's why I stay with her and do what I do."

Day 6

27th December 2014

07:05am

"My day's just started thanks to a wonderful phone that's dying on me and decided to run out of charge half way through the night, switch itself off and not let the alarm go off. That's more than a little irritating.

I've just got up to the dulcet tones of my sons' piano playing "Santa Clause is Coming to Town". It could have been a lot worse.

I can hear Mum talking so I think she can hear the neighbours kids and she thinks it's my son. I'm just making her a cup of tea then I'll go straight up to her with some water and start the day.

I've got a few aches and pains today as well so it's going to be an interesting day. My back's hurting, chest is hurting. I think they're muscle pains. I think I must have twisted funny in bed or something. We'll see how things develop."

I have already indicated that I am no stranger to pain. I actually have an unusually high pain threshold. It is, however, a fact that for the past eight years or more not a single day has passed where I have been pain free. For the most part the pains are little more than an aggravation, occasionally however they will present with greater intensity and demand more of my energy and concentration to continue working through them.

Anyone who lives with constant pain will tell you that it causes a huge amount of fatigue. In that I am no different to anyone else. Pain and stress are for me the most exhausting elements of everything I deal with in this environment. Ultimately what keeps me pushing through is the constant knowledge that three people are acutely dependent upon me to remain upright and functioning. No pressure then.

08:15am

> ***"The Care team have arrived and are upstairs now with Mum. I'm going to get some washing up done.***
>
> ***I don't think Mum's going to be getting up today. I wouldn't expect her to and I'm not going to push her in any particular direction.***
>
> ***It could be an interesting day today. Apparently all the roads are really icy and it's difficult getting through so we might have some delays with the Care Team. But we'll see how it goes.***
>
> ***Idiot me left the slow cooker on all night so the stew is a little bit over cooked now unfortunately. It is still edible. It'll still do lunch for me and my partner."***

Dealing with a Care Agency requires a certain amount of flexibility where the timing is concerned. Any number of things can affect the teams' schedule. From simple traffic conditions to a major medical emergency with another client. Of all of those things however, weather is the worst and most unpredictable factor.

It is, however, far more manageable in a city environment than it is in a rural one. There were occasions in Scotland when the Carers were unable to reach us at all, either for a certain shift or possibly even an entire day.

This is, for me, another reason why I feel I should know as much as I can about my mothers' condition. Should the need arise I do have the knowledge and capabilities to do what is required in the Care Teams absence. It is not something I relish doing, but, in emergency situations I am capable. The knowledge of this fact alone provides me with a certain sense of security which is invaluable in this situation.

09:20am

"The Carers have gone. Mum's stayed in bed as predicted. She's still complaining of nauseous, sickly feelings but I've taken up her breakfast, a cup of tea. She's settled down watching the weekend telly. She doesn't look too bad actually. Her fluid output by this morning was looking a lot better than yesterday so we'll see how we go.

We've had a shopping delivery this morning which I didn't know was coming. I knew it was coming today, I just didn't know it was coming first thing. The little man has been an absolute angel helping me to take it through to the kitchen. It's so sweet watching him carrying those bags and he wants to be so helpful. He gets so much pleasure out of it. It's the sweetest thing to watch.

I've put all the shopping away and now I can start relaxing a little bit I think. My partner is still in bed. It is starting to irritate. That's three days in a row she hasn't got up before ten o'clock, and only then because I've got her up. I'm starting to feel like she's taking the piss a little bit. It's fine having a lie-in every once in a while. I won't ever get

one but I've got no problem giving her a lie-in every once in a while. I've got a problem because she's doing virtually nothing around the house, complaining of being tired all the time, then she's the first one to bed and she's the last one up. All of that doesn't balance for me. I know she gets fatigued but there's a point where I just can't accommodate it and she is reaching that point. I'm going to have to have words with her today.

I'll let her get up but she's got to start helping out a bit more. This is the busiest time of the year and she's let me do the whole thing on my own for three days straight now."

One of my biggest problems is that I often forget that other people are not like me. They do not operate the same way I do. They do not have the same capabilities that I have. I know this all sounds incredibly arrogant, but it is true.

I know I am capable of functioning for incredibly long periods of time on very little sleep. I don't like doing it but, when it is necessary then I will simply push through pain and sleep barriers and "soldier on" as the saying goes. For me this is natural. I've been doing it all my life. Naturally then I expect that everyone else can do just the same. Obviously this is not the case. My expectations of other people are simply too high and I mean no disrespect when I say that.

In my partners case her condition makes this even more relevant. The intellectual side of me knows that my partner needs so much more sleep than I do yet whatever is left of the emotional side of me rails at the apparent weakness that she displays around me. It is unfair of me, I know this. Unfortunately that knowledge doesn't always help.

11:35am

"Everyone's up now. I got my partner up at ten o'clock. She's been keeping the little one company. He does like

his new little train set, which is nice, even though it is a bitch to put together, but it is fun watching him play with it. It is nice to see there are things he likes to play with.

All in all, a pretty good day so far. I'm just about to make Mum her lunch. I've had a little chat with my partner about her morning time-keeping which she's taken pretty well. Hopefully I wasn't over-forbearing but something had to be said. It's just nice to feel like I'm getting some support, in the morning especially.

So I'm going to give Mum her lunch then convince my partner to have hers and hopefully we'll have a good afternoon."

Another one of the issues related to my partners' condition is her eating habits. Left to her own devices she can easily forget to eat. Breakfast and lunchtimes are especially challenging in this regard. It is a strange thing for me to get my head around because I struggle to believe that she never gets hungry. The fact is that, once food is presented to her she virtually inhales it, she eats so fast. I think it is simply the act of preparing it that she has an issue with. To my mind this is a combination of the general fatigue that she suffers from coupled with a severe lack of motivation.

In this regard, having Mum with us has actually proven helpful. I am now in a position where I cook a major meal daily and I generally cook enough so that there are left-overs for the next day. This means that, with minimal effort on the part of my partner she can now benefit from two solid cooked meals each day. Of course that increases my workload somewhat, but I guess everything has its price.

12:35pm

"Mum's had her lunch. She did a lot better with it today than she did yesterday. Maybe her appetite is coming back a little bit, which is good. She's doing O.K., still a

little bit woozy but she's happy watching her "Carry On" films. I think she's comfortable here. I think she's happy that she's here and not in the nursing home anymore. So that's a result. I'm just waiting for the care Team to turn up and look after her for the lunchtime and then I'll get myself some food."

01:40pm

"The girls have been and gone. They're struggling at the moment because they are short staffed over Christmas and the weather is knocking people out as well, so the timings have been a little bit off today. But that's not a big problem for us here.

Either mum is not drinking enough or she is retaining too much fluid, either way her output is lower than it should be and it's still quite dark. That's worrying in its own right. We'll just have to see how she goes over this weekend and then figure out what's happening from Monday regarding B12 and possibly getting the Doctor out to pay another visit and see what we can do. We'll play this one by ear, day by day. Her colour's not too bad but, we'll see.

In the meantime my partner is finally having something to eat. It's only taken me three and a half hours to convince her to actually get some food.

Now that the girls have been, I'm going to get myself some lunch."

You will have probably noticed by now that, when it comes to food I am generally the last person I think about. It would be natural to assume that the reason for this is that I place myself far lower in my priority list than everyone else. While that assumption is basically correct in general terms, it is not actually the reason behind my actions in this case. In simplest terms, the reason here is actually the opposite, selfishness.

You see, I like to take my time with food. I do not like to be rushed, I do not like to be disturbed when I am eating and I do like peace and quiet in which to enjoy my meal. In this situation that can only really be achieved once everyone else in the house has been seen to first. Essentially, by making sure that everyone else has had what they need and they are comfortable and relaxed, I have effectively bought myself a small window of opportunity when I can almost ignore my surroundings, relax and eat.

03:30pm

"Mum's asleep upstairs, my son is asleep downstairs, I'm getting the evening meal prepared, I've got the roast in. I'm about to start working on the rest of it. I don't know how much Mum will eat. I'm pretty sure I know how much my partner will eat (as much as I put in front of her). She's looking forward to it.

It's been a quiet day, a peaceful day for the most part. I'm tired. I really must have twisted and turned funny in my sleep last night. I've got pains, quite severe pains all up the top of my back, across my chest. They're muscle pains but it doesn't help the cause. But it could be worse."

05:20pm

"The food is done, everyone's been fed. I even got to eat this time which is quite a novelty these days. My son, after a lot of encouragement, actually joined me at the table for some food. It's a weird one this. We've been trying to get him to eat solid meals for ages and he resists. Every once in a while he has a real taste for real food, but tonight was kind of strange.

Initially I took his plate in and he wasn't interested. Now, in the past that has bothered me, especially when I've

done the cooking but, I tried a new tactic today. We'd put the table up so I sat at the table with my meal. I brought his plate back to the table and put it in front of an empty chair next to me and left it there. He kept coming to and from the table, showing a little bit of interest, more curiosity and then saying no and walking away. I didn't apply any pressure at all. Every time he came close to the table I encouraged him, I smiled, I played with him. Eventually it paid dividends. He started by picking up a little bit of sweetcorn off his plate, tasting that. Then a bit more. Then he asked for a spoon and, while he didn't eat all of the food off the plate by any means, he had two helpings of sweetcorn, he ate some green beans. I'd class that as a success. He walked away from the table happy and the whole event was not stressful for him which it has been in the past. Trying to get him to eat can be stressful. All in all I class that as a result. A very positive one.

In a minute I'm going to go check up on Mum, see how she's done with her food and then it'll be another hour or so before the Girls arrive to settle Mum in for the night, and another day will slowly draw to a close."

Even a child who does not have additional challenges can be a difficult prospect at meal times. Personally I think the key is to take the stress out of the event. Meal times have to be seen as fun times. I don't care at the moment if my son eats with his fingers or with a utensil. I don't care if he keeps coming backwards and forwards between the table and the television. I don't care if he eats everything on his plate. What I do care about is that he eats something, enjoys it and walks away from the experience with a smile on his face. All the other details can be sorted out gradually over time.

I never had a good relationship with food as either a child or a young adult. In fact it is only really in the last ten years or so that my relationship with food has started to improve. The reason for this was simple. As a child meal times were terrifying experiences thanks to a Father that had no clue and was incredibly violent in his ignorance. I hated cabbage as a child (and I think that's a pretty common phenomenon) but my father insisted that I eat it, even going so far as to provide an entire plateful as my Sunday dinner. If I didn't eat it then I was beaten and I would simply go hungry. Is it any wonder then that I had no interest in family meals growing up and food in general did not evoke any pleasurable emotions in me?

This is not what I want for my son so I choose to take a relaxed approach to the whole thing. When he chooses to eat I praise him enthusiastically and when he doesn't I don't stress about it. It is a slow process but we have seen definite improvements in our sons eating habits over the years, so I guess we must be doing something right.

06:55pm

"My son has just gone up to say goodnight to his Grandma and go to bed.

Mum did better with her food tonight although, she complained about the sprouts, she said they were cooked awful which is kind of interesting because I never cooked any. I never put any on her plate. So that was an interesting discussion. But, apart from that we're doing O.K.

I'm just waiting for the Girls to arrive now to settle Mum down. I should be doing the washing up but I'm a bit tired so I'm going to leave it until later. I'm going to have a proper sit down and a rest after the girls have been and watch something, I'll get the washing up done after.

My partner seems pretty happy with her birthday. A quiet day, a peaceful day. She likes her presents. I guess I shouldn't expect more than that. There'll come a time when I can make my partners day a special day. A proper,

special day. Because she is special. Oh I know I gripe. She doesn't do this, she doesn't do that but at the end she probably has the same gripes about me in one way or another. Yet despite all our individual failings we love each other and we're still together even with everything that's going on around us. I guess that's got to say something."

At the best of times relationships can be incomprehensible entities to me. I struggle with them. I have low tolerance of other people and I really struggle to understand what I call the "gentler" emotions, love, happiness, contentment. These concepts may as well have come from Mars for all the understanding I have of them. I guess I spent so much of my life locking all of those emotions away, mainly due to an up-bringing that did not encourage that level of feeling. It is only in later years that I have started to unpack those old emotional boxes and take a look inside. Understanding is slow, but I think I am getting there.

In the meantime, one of the things these past three years of looking after my Mum has given me is patience. It is by no means perfect. There are still times when I want to scream in frustration. But, for the most part I can stay balanced and focused enough to allow me to take the time necessary to understand those closest to me.

09:10pm

"My partner has gone to bed. I've been up to check up on Mum. She enjoyed her mince pies and her Baileys. I took another cup of tea up to her. Hopefully she'll start settling off in an hour or so. She's watching "Sherlock" at the moment, she's half way through that so she may well drop off in the next hour.

As for me, I've still got to tidy the kitchen and wash up. I really need to tidy up in the living room as well because that looks like a bomb's hit it. At some point I've got to work out when I can get a hoover 'round there. Christ

knows when that's going to be. Then I'm going to look towards getting some R&R and then going to bed at some point."

So, my Mum is on medication, lots of medication, and I'm giving her alcohol. How bad am I? How irresponsible?

That is what some people would think. Fortunately for Mum I am not one of them. You see I don't believe that half a centimetre of baileys in a tumbler is going to have a massive negative impact on my Mother even with all the medication she is on. Quite the opposite in fact. It gives her some pleasure and, as I've already noted, she has precious few things in her life right now that give her pleasure. Ultimately I don't see my role as keeping Mum alive for the longest time possible at the exclusion of all else. I view it as providing for my Mother the best quality of life that I can for as long as she is able to appreciate it. Occasionally that is going to mean bending the rules a little. This is one of those occasions.

10.45pm

"I've just been up to settle Mum down for the night. She's finished off her cup of tea. She's finished watching "Sherlock" so she can get some rest now. I switched off her T.V., switched off her light, said goodnight, brought the cups downstairs and made the executive decision that I can't be arsed to wash up tonight. As much as I hate to have that as my first job in the morning, that's what's going to happen. I'm just too goddamn tired to think about it right now.

So I'm just going to lie down and chill with an episode of "Marvel – Agents of Shield" for an hour. Unwind my brain and then off to bed for me.

The house still looks like a bomb site but I just can't do anything with it. I'll sort it tomorrow.

> ***I've also got to decide what I'm going to cook tomorrow. I think I'm going to do something simple. If I do a simple pasta dish tomorrow it's going to be a lot easier and save me a lot of time which I can use elsewhere on getting some of the house cleaned up and all that kind of stuff. But we'll see how things go. At the moment I'm sensing a carbonara is in the offing tomorrow."***

There enough hours in the day. I imagine that's a complaint a lot of people make regardless of their personal situation. I do, however, genuinely believe that, were I never to sleep I still would not get everything done that I wanted to do. The every-day tasks just seem to pile up continuously at a rate that is truly alarming. I'm starting to develop a real appreciation for the guy who paints the Forth Bridge. There is a sense of futility to the whole thing that can sometimes feel quite overwhelming.

Day 7

28th December 2014

06:20am

> ***"I've been up ten or fifteen minutes. I did not want to get up today and my alarm doesn't seem to be working on my phone which is wonderful. Thankfully my partners' went off so I was coaxed awake by the wonderful tunes of "The Grinch". Somehow appropriate when you look at me.***
>
> ***I'm still in quite a bit of pain across my shoulders and the top of my chest. I'm ridiculously tired.***
>
> ***My son is already awake. I'm not getting him up yet but I will soon. I need my time. I need to wake up first. Then start a new day."***

Pain and fatigue are cumulative. This is something I know to be true. I also know that I am supposed to take the time to look after myself in this situation. How do I know this? Because every professional I encounter keeps telling me, that's how. The thing is, that is very easy to say. Doing it, well, that's another thing entirely.

I am only too aware that I am pushing myself physically and mentally harder than I have ever done in the past. I know too that this will ultimately have a price. If I continue as I am going there will come a time when my body will simply quit, hand in its' proverbial notice and bid me a not so fond farewell.

07:10am

"Mum's awake, she's got a cup of tea, her juice, I've given here her morning pills and she says she feels a little bit better than she has the last couple of days, which is good. However, she has been getting quite painful spasms which causes me some concern. It's something we're both familiar with, an issue revolving around the catheter which I'll have to keep an eye on today. If it gets any worse then I'll have to get the district nurses out. We shall see what happens. I'll have to get the Girls to check if Mum's bypassing again.

My son is up and awake and, again he's taken his nappy off. Thankfully it doesn't look like he's wet the bed, still, I haven't had the chance to check properly. I might see if I can convince Hannah to do that. But he's happy. He went straight in to say good morning to Nana, spotted the T.V. and became hypnotised. He's now happily ensconced on the sofa with a bottle, his raisins and the T.V.. So he's a happy boy.

While my partner did wake up to her alarm enough to turn it off and talk to me a little bit, I don't anticipate seeing her for a little while. But you never know, she might surprise me. We shall see."

To call the District Nurse or not to call the District Nurse, that is the question. And a damn tricky one it is too. I tend to be really proactive where my Mum's health is concerned. I am not in the habit of letting things fester for too long before taking remedial action.

I am probably a major irritant to the District Nurses and possibly the local G.P. as well because I do get them out the instant I feel something is not right with my mother. After three years of doing this I am only too well aware of how serious little things can become and how quickly. As far as I am concerned it is the definition of my job that I do everything in my power to ensure that Mum stays out of hospital wherever possible. If that means I have to get professionals out to her more often than they would perhaps prefer then that is exactly what I will do.

09:30am

"The Carers have all been and gone, and what an interesting start to the day that's been. One of the girls turned up with a raging cold. She knew she shouldn't be here. She told me at the outset that she had this cold, knowing full well what my response would be. There was no way she was going to go up and see Mum.

She shouldn't have been working today. She knows that. I know that. I understand why she was, but we'll get to that another time.

I then phone the care agency to get some officious, idiotic, disrespectful oik on the phone who ultimately ends up hanging up on me because she does not like the way I'm talking to her. Bearing in mind I wasn't using offensive language. I was agitated and I was brutally honest and you see, that's the thing in this country that people can't stand is when you're being honest with them.

I have no problems making a formal complaint about that woman and the agency. I'm really not happy. I'm in the same position I was in in Scotland. Care Agencies it seems country wide, they have great staff working for them. The staff are not supported by a management system that can function correctly and with any sense of purpose. They are not supported with any quantifiably useful training. And

they are not supported by a rate of pay that reflects the work that they do, or even conditions that reflect the work that they do. It's about time that started to change.

Care agencies charge exorbitant fees, for what I don't know. They're making money hand over fist out of the industry of looking after people. And they're not doing the job right. And it's not because the staff can't do the job right, it's because the staff aren't being trained right, and the agencies don't care. All they're interested in is their profit margin.

Now I don't begrudge any business a profit. What I do begrudge is that business making an exorbitant profit whilst not providing a quality service. That's starting to become my mission I think. I'm tired of having to deal with shoddy service from the management aspect of businesses in the care industry. That's going to stop.

The net result was, I sent one Carer up to my Mum to start doing what she could without putting herself or my Mum in any danger, under the instructions that if she needed any further assistance then I would jump in. Had that happened the Care Agency itself would have been looking at a real roasting. As it is I am going to be getting hold of the C.Q.C. (Care Quality Commission) and I will be making a formal complaint about the agency. Both about their staffing levels over this period and about the way they have behaved in this particular instance.

I don't believe in second chances in this industry. Too many people get second, third, fourth and fifth chances which is why the industry does not get regulated the way it needs to be. It does not get the legislation it needs. And the people who work in the industry do not get the respect they deserve. This is going to change.

As a result of all this, I'm well behind on my work now. By now I should have got the washing up done. I should have got all my cleaning done ready to start thinking about heading towards lunch time. As it is I've got none of that done so I've got to do that now. I'm going to have a stressful couple of hours ahead now, trying to get everything completed in time to be able to serve Mum lunch.

A positive today. My partner got up, just after eight o'clock which is good. I didn't have to go and rouse her. Mum's feeling, not too bad. She's got her breakfast. She's got a cup of tea. She's stayed in bed still. I think she's going to stay in bed until she gets the B12 which is not a situation I like but there's no way around it. She doesn't have the energy levels without it."

Well that was quite a rant, wasn't it? As you might have guessed after reading that, I was a tad angry. That anger however, does not invalidate anything I said at the time. Upon reflection that is still my considered opinion. Both in terms of my comments towards the care Agency itself and the industry in general.

There was a time when caring for the elderly and infirm was a worthy thing to do. It seems those times are long gone. I sometimes feel that garbage collectors get higher levels of respect and better working conditions than those who work in the care industry. The management of Care Agencies seem purely focused on their "bottom line". Little interest seems to be shown in either the needs of their clients or the conditions of their employees and unfortunately, it seems that current legislation supports their position.

When I reflect on some of the events I've witnessed over the past three years since looking after my mother I find myself ashamed to call myself a member of the human race. This is one area where we have seriously lost our way, both as a nation and as a species.

11:15am

"I'm just about to check on Mum again and then I'll be starting to make her lunch.

I've had another one of those conversations with my partner this morning about what she's not doing. I've tried to be as gentle as I can with her but she recognises that, especially over the past week and a half, she's not really been doing anything. And she should be. I will make allowances for her condition, but only so far. She has responsibilities. She's made choices here the same as I have, and one of those choices ultimately has been to remain a part of this family unit, and that means that she has to do her share.

I hate having these conversations with her. I hate the feeling that I'm always getting at her. I try not to, but, at the end of the day, if I don't say anything she'll never know how I feel and that's not a basis for a good relationship.

I wish things were easier. I wish I was never in this position. But I am and I've had to make choices and, yes, those choices have had an impact on everyone in my family. But I'm doing what I always do, which is my best, for all concerned.

Choices. Everyone tries to avoid them, especially the more challenging ones. It's understandable to a point. No-one likes to put themselves into difficult or unpleasant situations. Unfortunately life is all about choices.

I used to be the same as everyone else. I used to shy away from the tough call, hide myself away in the hopes that time would make the choice unnecessary. But I've learnt over the years that time does nothing more than make the eventual choice more impacting. The longer you stay in indecision the tougher the consequences are likely to get.

Now I have a very simple decision making process. I never look too far ahead at potential consequences because they may never happen. My decisions are based purely on the immediate. Is it important for me now? Is it necessary that I undertake a certain action at this point in time? Whatever consequences may occur will be dealt with in the fullness of time.

I have heard a few times of a story about a man on the top floor of a burning building. The only way to escape the fire is to jump out of the window. If he stays in the building he will certainly die. If he jumps he may also die, but that is not decided. Between the moment he jumps from the window to the moment he hits the ground there are, potentially, a million events that can occur which could alter the outcome. Of course, until the man jumps he will never know. Most people will stick with what they know and stay in the building even though they know they will die. The uncertainty involved in jumping out of the window would simply be too much. My life has been replete with uncertainty from the day I was born. It is all I know. Me, I'd jump.

11:50am

"Mum's got her lunch, she's had her lunch-time medication. I made her a cup of tea but then she decided she didn't want a cup of tea, she wanted a glass of milk, so I swapped that out.

Then my son decided he was hungry so I offered him some scrambled eggs and he said "Oh, yes please!", so I made him some scrambled eggs. The moment they hit the plate, he decided he didn't want them. He's in one of those moods today where he's not going to tell you what he wants, everything you offer him he's going to say no to and then he's going to cry and play tantrums with you the whole time. It's not what I really want today, or any day

for that matter but today especially when I'm not having the best start to the day as it is. It's really not making me feel brilliant.

There are many times I wish I was somewhere else, I really do. Anywhere other than here. I do love the three people I'm looking after but I know I'm not the right person to be looking after them. I'm just all they've got."

Doubt and depression form an integral part of my existence these days. Admittedly this is not helped by the bi-polar. I will always question the correctness of what I am doing where my family is concerned. There will frequently be times when I wonder if they could do better with someone else in my place.

It is not arrogance that keeps me doing what I am doing it is simply the absolute knowledge that were I not here there would be nobody else to fill my shoes and step up to the plate on their behalf.

I have a skill set and knowledge base that makes me perfectly suited to some of the key elements of this situation but I also have a temperament that is woefully inadequate. This is something I am painfully aware of and I do take great pains to keep that side of me under tight control. Unfortunately that only adds to the total work load and stress.

02:20pm

"The girls came and went as normal, I've had lunch since they've gone. I was going to have a lie down, I'm really tired again, but as it's worked out, by the time I finished lunch it was nearly two o'clock and it just didn't seem worth it. I'd be getting myself up at three anyway.

Mum's had herself a little nap. I'm going to go up and check on her in a minute. I've finished the rest of the washing up now so everything's clear for me to make

more mess in about an hour and a half. I am going to go simple tonight with the cooking and do a basic carbonara, except I'll be making my own sauce for it. We shall see how we go.

The little one has been very energetic today. He's been demanding lots of attention, keeping my partner busy. My partner actually offered to do the rest of the washing up but the little one's just been so demanding so I let my partner keep him occupied and I finished what I started.

Almost the end of another week."

03:20pm

"Mum was a little peckish this afternoon so she's had a couple of biscuits, another cup of tea, she hasn't slept too much which is actually quite good. She's a bit more perky today. A bit more interested in the world, certainly more interested in her food which is a plus.

I'm going to go up in a minute and give her her afternoon tablet and then start thinking about preparing the evening meal soon. Well, it'll be afternoon/evening. Maybe my son will even try a bit, you never know."

Mums' eating habits have always been a very good indicator of the state of her health. When her appetite begins to go then I start to worry. That is the beginning of a downward spiral that can escalate with incredible speed.

I never usually worry for the first couple of days because, let's face it, everyone can have off days. But, if it persists then it does become a cause for concern. It's a simple chain of events to follow. If Mum doesn't eat then she starts to get tired. The more tired she becomes, the less she feels like eating and so the circle is complete. Eventually it begins to affect everything, especially her fluid intake and when that starts to drop then I really start to worry.

Failing appetite is definitely one of those things with Mum that I try and "nip in the bud" as soon as possible.

04:00pm

"I've just been up, checked in on Mum, emptied her bin and refreshed it. Then I stayed up there for a bit of a "chinwag".

Mum was reminiscing days of old, back when it was just me, my brother and her, some of the things we used to get up to.

This is kind of difficult for me. Mum talks about events that happened. Funny, not funny, all kinds of things. But they're events that, with the best will in the world, I can't draw to memory, I can't see. It's weird. It's like when I look at photographs. It's almost like I'm looking at people that I recognise but they don't depict events that I can see in my head. I may be technically in the photograph but I've no memory of the event. I've no memory of the occurrence that prompted the photograph. And these conversations with Mum evoke similar feelings. They're a little bit surreal.

But I think that's one of the things, especially this past year, that Mum misses the most since the stroke, or my Mum needs the most since the stroke, is this support of family, support of recollection. In the nursing home there was no-one to really talk to in this way and that was difficult for Mum.

I know she likes seeing all of the fun and games that my son gets up to which is why I'm a bit annoyed that circumstances have led to the fact that, almost this entire

past week Mum's been in bed. Because really she should have been up, she should have been in her wheelchair, she should have been downstairs with us, she should have been able to watch my son playing and play with him to a point. But she hasn't been able to do that and if ever there was a time to do it, it would have been Christmas.

I wanted to give Mum a really, really memorable Christmas, and I haven't. Not by my standards, and that's hard.

My past is very much a closed book to me. I have little glimpses of certain events, snapshot images that pop into my head from time to time, but no real recollection of things. So I get uncomfortable when Mum starts regaling old stories to me. These are the times when I wish our Step-Dad was still here. It would be at times like this that he would prove his worth more than any other. He would sit with her and listen to her and enjoy the memories that she wants to share with him whereas I just get uncomfortable and immediately start looking for excuses to leave. These are the times when I really doubt my value to my Mum.

06:10pm

"The food's done, everyone's eaten. Despite Mum prophesising that she wasn't going to be hungry and that she was feeling nauseous she still did pretty well with her meal. She said she enjoyed it and had about three quarters of the plate. I'm not going to complain at that.

As for the little lamb, he passed out at about four o'clock and he's still asleep so I've put a bit on one side for him. He will or won't eat when he's ready.

And me and my partner, we did something we've not done in a long, long time. We actually sat down at the table together and had a nice meal and talked. It was kind of a

novel, unique and eminently pleasurable experience. All in all, not bad. I can live with the way the day has gone for the most part.

Now I just wait for the girls to turn up to settle Mum down for the night. My partner said she'll wash up tonight. There's not a huge amount but it would be nice if she did. I'm impossibly tired today. I'm going to make another attempt at getting into bed before midnight. How well that's going to work out, God only knows.

The traditional family meal around a table has never really featured too heavily in my life. It's not something I'm used to. But I can understand the appeal. It provides the perfect opportunity for family socialisation and it is definitely something I want to encourage as we move forward, especially for my son. Apart from anything else it may well improve his eating habits.

I don't want my son to grow up with the same lack of understanding and appreciation for family that I always had as a child. I want him to feel safe and loved and part of something very special. Having not really had that myself I know how important it is.

08:00pm

"The carers have been and gone. Mum's settled down for the night. She's actually quite tired, I don't think she'll stay awake too long tonight. But she's settled down with a mince pie, a cup of tea and "Only Fools and Horses".

The little one is refusing to go to sleep, but then, he can hear everything going on across the hallway and he's too inquisitive for his own good, that little thing. We'll see how he settles.

My partner's done the washing up which I'm really grateful for. We've got a cup of tea and we actually have

some time. So, there's nothing much on the telly, we're going to sit down and break out Monopoly. It'll be nice to do something fun."

It was always going to be one of the major challenges when looking at the call times for the Care Team. My son goes to bed at seven o'clock every night. This meant that if the care Team were to arrive later than that, say eight or nine o'clock then they would, almost certainly, wake him up. In that respect my son takes after me. Once he is awake, he is awake. It would take hours to settle him back down again.

Therefore I decided to have the last call from the Carers at the same time as my sons bedtime. Yes, it meant that he would almost never settle off immediately but, when he did eventually settle he would stay settled as there would be no further disturbances to wake him.

Balancing the needs of all three of my charges is always the constant challenge that I face every single day. It definitely keeps me on my toes, at least when it's not driving me to distraction.

10:30pm

"My partner has taken herself off to bed. What can I say? Monopoly was fun, while it lasted. It took her just about an hour to royally whoop my ass. She plays like my daughter does. Not that I'm a sore looser or anything.

Anyway after that we decided to curl up on the sofa, watch an episode of "D.I.Y. S.O.S. – The Big Build", I love that show. Yeh, she's gone off up to bed and I'm going to chill for another hour or so on the computer, catch up with my e-mails and things, and then get myself to bed for around midnight. All in all, a pretty good day.

My partner's done the washing up so, I'm looking around and there's little to nothing for me to do in the kitchen. She's done a bit of tidying up in the living room so that's

looking a lot better now. I can actually go to bed tonight with the feeling that I'm not waking up to a complete bomb site tomorrow on top of everything else which is more than a little pleasing.

Of course I've still got the issues to resolve with Mum regarding her B12. Tomorrow's Monday so it's time to get on to the District Nurses, the G.P.s so we can start nailing this on the head and start getting Mum back to some sort of higher energy level, then hopefully start getting her back downstairs and with the family again. Then maybe we'll be in a position to start the New Year properly. Fingers' crossed. We shall see."

Afterword

I should probably now mention that, at the time of writing this, the issue with my Mums' B12 has kind of been resolved, just not to anyone's satisfaction.

It turns out that Mums' B12 levels were actually fine, as were all of her other results. This means that a lack of B12 was not the reason behind Mums' continued lethargy . The problem we now face is that we don't know what is causing it.

So that was a week in my life and the life of my family. It was Christmas but, to be honest, the weeks before and the weeks since have all been pretty much the same so, aside from cooking a few roasts and receiving a few gifts there is not really that much to tell them apart.

As I draw this all to a close I am left with the overriding question, why? Why did I write this in the first place? What did I hope to achieve? In the beginning I thought it might be useful to people to really understand what it is that I do on a daily basis. Not so that I could garner sympathy or anything like that, just plain, simple understanding. However, as I got deeper and deeper into this project I found that there was definitely a kind of therapy for me in the process.

I am not one given to talking too much about what I feel. Yet, for some reason, I find that I have no problem writing about my feelings. In the end this process has proven to be quite therapeutic for me. It has enabled me to unload a few emotional demons onto the pages in a way I would never have felt comfortable doing in a conversation.

If you, the reader, have made it this far then I admire your patience and perseverance, and I thank you.

Dedication

Throughout the course of this diary there has been one person who has barely featured. This is not because I do not love her or consider her to be a part of my family because, on both counts, I absolutely do. She has not featured simply because she does not live with me and, as such was not involved in the events of this past week.

That person is my daughter and I would like to take this opportunity to tell her how much she means to me, how much I love her and how much I am grateful to her for giving me a second chance at being a Father.

I know I do not see you as often as either one of us would like at the moment, and I know you understand the reasons why that is the case. But, even when I am not by your side I still think of you, I miss you and I will always love you.

CPSIA information can be obtained at www.ICGtesting.com
Printed in the USA
LVOW04s2041080515

437783LV00034B/1391/P